T

THE INDIAN FERMENT

A TRAVELLER'S TALE

H.G. Alexander

Introduction by
C.F. Andrews

ThreeRivers
PUBLISHERS
in association with
Westland Ltd

Three Rivers Publishers
2nd Floor, 6 Eastern Avenue, Maharani Bagh,
New Delhi 110 065

westland ltd
61, Silverline Building, Alapakkam Main Road, Maduravoyal, Chennai 600 095
No. 38/10 (New No.5), Raghava Nagar, New Timber Yard Layout, Bangalore 560 02
23/181, Anand Nagar, Nehru Road, Santacruz East, Mumbai 400 055
93, 1st Floor, Sham Lal Road, Daryaganj, New Delhi 110 002

www.westlandbooks.in

The Indian Ferment is published in the Indian subcontinent by Three Rivers Publisher in association with westland ltd 2013

10 9 8 7 6 5 4 3 2 1

ISBN 978-93-82618-41-6

Set in Bembo Std 11.5/14.5
Typeset by Eleven Arts, Delhi 110 035
Printed by Raj Press, New Delhi

PREFACE

India, like the figures of her gods, is a land with many faces. A few are known to the West; many remain unknown. This is a traveller's sketch-book, nothing more. My journey of exploration led me into strange jungles of racial suspicion and misunderstanding. Without one Indian language I could not penetrate very far; and yet I believe I learnt enough for the record of my experiences to be worth publishing—though I wrote without intending to publish.

It has been necessary to revise rather freely the letters I wrote; but I have tried to be faithful to the impression of the time. Consequently the reader will find strong judgments written in the heat of particular moments; but, if he will be patient, he may find qualifications later, when I learnt more. I believe it is well to leave the record of these strong impressions—both those critical of Indians and those critical of Europeans. Alone they do not make a true picture; but the picture is not true without them.

No words can express my debt to all, especially to my Indian friends and hosts, who helped in my Eastern education. Many busy men and women turned aside at a moment's notice to answer questions and to show friendship. I do not know that I have ever met such openness to an English traveller as I found everywhere in India; and this is the more remarkable as this confidence has lately been abused.

All those friends I thank; one I mention by name, Tarini Prasad Sinha. To him, and to the friendship of his country and mine, I dedicate this book.

INTRODUCTION

After reading carefully again and again this writing of Horace Alexander's, I felt very strongly, indeed, that it ought to be published, because it has given with remarkably keen observation a description of the ferment of thought in India and the racial feeling aroused.

It is supremely necessary to appreciate this Indian ferment in England at once, in order that a great calamity may be avoided. For unless especially the younger generation in England, which should naturally sympathize with Young India in its present revolutionary mood, can understand what is taking place, there may be perpetrated once more in our own times one of those ghastly tragedies of human history not altogether dissimilar from that which took place in Ireland just after the War.

For the one question that perplexes the soul of Young India to-day is not at all whether freedom is immediately to be achieved or not. Already that has been decided in the affirmative by every Indian who has thought over the matter. The burning question to-day is this: whether freedom is to be obtained by violent means or by non-violent means. Even the much less important question, as to whether this freedom should involve complete separation from England, or the maintenance of some such loose connection as the Dutch and British in South Africa still retain, will depend for its own answer almost entirely on the solution of this larger problem about violence; because it follows in direct moral sequence that if the Indian Revolution, which has now actually begun, becomes wholly violent in character, it will engender on both sides a racial hatred that must finally lead to a severance from England both outward and inward.

For in that case there will arise complete antipathy of *spirit*, which is infinitely more serious than any outward severance of political relations.

My own attitude from first to last has been this: On the one hand, I have again and again declared that "independence" and "freedom" are synonymous terms, in their moral connotation, and that no true Englishman could ever wish to keep another people in bondage. On the other hand, I have also learned wholeheartedly to detest the murderous violence which is quite inextricably involved in modern war. It has come to me, as a life experience, and not as a mere dogma, that evil can never be overcome by evil, but only by good. It need hardly be said, in England, that this is nothing except Christ's own teaching. It need also hardly be told, in India, that this is nothing except the teaching of the Buddha. Yet so little is this teaching followed in both countries in modern times that, in season and out of season, in India and Europe alike, this and this alone at the present juncture has become the one doctrine that I have felt it necessary at all costs to uphold. Indeed, I have been prepared at any moment to suffer for its truth, and have already done so.

It has been necessary for me thus to define my own position, while writing this Introduction, because there is no possibility for anyone who loves India to remain neutral to-day when these vital political questions are raised. For the time being, the foreign issue with regard to England and Swaraj is the most acute of all; but it carries with it an internal reformation in the wake of the political ferment. The hopefulness of the present situation is this: that as long as the present ferment continues to excite the masses of the people, who were sluggish and stagnant before, social changes of very far-reaching importance are bound to follow in order to correspond with the new political ideas. This has been witnessed to-day in its unrestricted form in Modern Turkey, but in a far more restricted way it is evident in India also.

The gravest of all dangers for the Administration at such a crisis is timidity. While it would be absurd to charge the eminent British statesmen who are still at the head of Indian affairs (for actual *self*-government in India has gone only a very little way forward) with a desire for reaction in social reform in India, yet the charge of timidity is by no means so lightly brushed aside; for there is a profound ignorance in these matters in London, as each Indian debate in both Houses of Parliament painfully reveals. Such ignorance leads to uncertainty of handling. This was acutely evident in the Bill proposed at Delhi last year for a reform, long overdue, dealing drastically with child marriage. Here the officials at Delhi, with the approval of the India Office in Whitehall, took the side of delay and caution—not from any lack of sympathy with Indian social reform, but through timidity as to the consequences involved. An abuse which Modern Turkey would have swept away in a single session is still allowed to linger on and fester.

It may very reasonably be argued that in a vast heterogeneous country such as India it is safer to err on the side of caution. To this I would answer that there are times when sitting on the safety-valve is not the best way of preventing the steam-boiler from bursting.

It is because Horace Alexander has realized so vividly the urgency of political reform in India, and along with this the need for the removal of the present racial and colour prejudices, which involve cruel insult and injustice, that I feel his vivid observations to be of special value at the present juncture. In one respect only it is embarrassing for me to write at his request, because I am frequently mentioned by him as an intimate, personal friend, and his praise is as generous as his friendship; but the extreme urgency of the matter makes diffidence on that account out of place. Things in India are much too critical for personal considerations to intervene.

After the amazing propaganda in the West of Miss Mayo's book, *Mother India,* and the bitterness which ensued, not only Mahatma Gandhi and the poet Rabindranath Tagore, but also Muhammadan and Sikh leaders in India, impressed upon me the necessity of going forward with all possible speed to Europe and America, in order to endeavour to create a better racial understanding. It is in this direct connection, and in order to fulfil their wishes, that I have ventured to press so strongly for Horace Alexander's manuscript to be published. There are impressions in it that would not correspond with my own opinions, but the freshness of observation is remarkable, and the perspective that the author has gained vividly represents in outline the picture of India in ferment to-day.

C. F. Andrews
Geneva

I

NAGPUR,
October 1927

On reaching a new country my first tendency is to use my eyes and to look at the country itself. This is partly because I am on the look-out for new birds; but also because I believe that the soul of a country is largely influenced by the natural surroundings: that is why big industrial cities have no soul. Appreciate the earth and the hills and trees and birds and insects and skies of India, and then you may begin to understand the people. Anyhow, that is my way—subconsciously.

There is not much "natural environment" to be seen in Bombay; but there is no lack of humanity. Only humanity in Bombay is no more of a guide to India than humanity in London is to England. You learn very quickly to harden your heart against the ghastly deformities the street beggars show in order to soften it; and you begin already to see from the thinness of the legs of the people you meet that most Indians are half-starved. Bombay is not a place where it is very easy to feel "unity with the whole creation".

After three or four days in Bombay I plunged into the real India—the agricultural district round Hoshangabad, in the Central Provinces, where English Quakers have had a mission for some fifty years. I left Bombay at night; so the first I saw of Indian country was not until we were well over the Ghats.

My first idea was that the country is absurdly like England. The patches of jungle we passed through were not alive with tigers and elephants, nor were they dark and dense with impenetrable creepers, nor the trees covered with gorgeous tropical flowers. It was a good deal like rather badly grown English copse-wood, with patches of green pasture here and there, and the country was pleasantly undulating like the English Midlands. Gradually it grew flatter and more open, with scattered bushes and much open grazing-ground, like a big English common, and occasional patches of cultivation: *Juara,* a tall thing like Indian corn, but with a totally different fruit; cotton, usually poor and thin, especially in contrast to the amazing crops in the Nile valley, but not as bad as the poor dried-up cotton in Greece; and one or two other things; the wheat-fields being all bare at present. I was appalled at the wastefulness of the cultivation. I got the impression of a country cultivated by very indifferent peasants who had not the faintest notion of manuring or any other part of modern agricultural science; and on the whole that idea is confirmed. The region round Itarsi is magnificent "black cotton" soil; they sow wheat on the same fields every year, without a thought of any manuring; and have now got to a sort of "rock bottom" annual yield, which is good under the circumstances. But the cultivators are all in the hands of the money-lenders. They can only work for seven or eight months in the year. It is suggested that the real purpose of Mr. Gandhi's spinning-wheel is to give the ryots something to occupy themselves with when otherwise they would be idle. Also it might keep them out of debt. But apparently it is almost an accepted custom to be in debt.

When I pointed to the vast amount of space that is wasted in poor pasture, I was first assured that all this was needed to support the cattle. This can hardly be true, and even it if were true it would be no defence. The attitude towards cattle seems to be rather like "the sanctity of human life" in the West. You may twist the tails of the cattle; you may beat them and prod them and neglect them, and starve them; but if you are guilty of the death of a cow, you have committed the greatest crime. I have seen a greater number of poor, diseased, starved cattle (to say nothing of dogs) since I reached India than I have ever seen before—and this is the best season of the year for them. Even in death their economic value is lost. Their bones, instead of making good manure for the fields of India, go to be used on the fields of England.

On my first evening at Itarsi we motored out into the jungle. We watched two or three parties of big, long-tailed monkeys with white faces; and we passed a "tiger shrine", where some time a man was killed by a tiger. We walked along by a stream in an open part of the jungle, which seemed like an English park gone wild, with splendid trees and open, grassy places. The trees are different from ours, though it happens that the one tree now in full flower, the teak, has a flower that looks like a Spanish chestnut. The spring is the time when the jungle is all on fire with brilliant blossom.

Naturally I was all eyes and ears for the new birds. When for years you have come to regard any new bird, even any unknown bird-call, as a rare event, scarcely to be expected even once a year, to be suddenly plunged into a world where every bird is new and every cry unknown, is exciting, and even rather upsetting. It is astonishingly difficult to see and identify birds about whose identity you have no clue. This is partly because of the foliage, but chiefly just unfamiliarity. I was quite pleased all at once to hear the note of a grey wagtail, and a few minutes later the sharp piping of a green sandpiper. It was reassuring to find that the birds have some real connection with England. The sight of a grey wagtail running by the stream was a solace to a home-sick wanderer.

An Indian jungle seems very different from what I had expected, but it has a peculiar loveliness of its own which I cannot describe. Flocks of green parrots go screaming among the tree-tops; other birds chatter or sing gently among the foliage; even the great grey hornbill can easily disappear among the big leaves. There is the noise of many insects, humming and rasping and buzzing. I am seeing India at its greenest, and it is almost as green as England. The lights are harder; there is no soft English haze. But the evening skies, often with great thunder-clouds, brilliantly lit on their summits, intensely black below, and, above them, immensely high, pink wisps of cloud, or intense gold and red streamers near the western horizon: these are sights to be long remembered.

I have written of the poor state of agriculture, at least as I have seen it. Unhappily, too, Young India does not seem yet to be really roused to action in the matter. There are only about a thousand students at the agricultural colleges, compared with, I suppose, ten thousand who study law. But I have met one of the thousand already, a pleasant Muslim youth, whose father, an official of Bhopal State, lives next door to the Friends' Mission House. The son is at the agricultural college at Cawnpore. His father asked me about the agricultural colleges in England, so of course I sang the praises of Wye. He said "a friend of his" was thinking of sending his son there. His own son seemed to know quite as much about Wye as I did; so I guessed it was he who wanted to go there. Afterwards I learnt that this was so, and they were already in correspondence with the Wye authorities. The son's ambition is to become an agricultural official in British India—not a bad ambition, perhaps. He was quite sure that he did not want to serve an Indian State.

I must tell about another hopeful thing—the school at Makoriya. From Itarsi R. G. took me one day to the village of Makoriya, whose people he advises and doctors once a week. The village is on the edge of the jungle; it was settled some years ago by the Friends' Mission. Christians, Hindus, Muslims, and aboriginals live close together, but each in their own section of the village. The thatched cottages—most of them so low that the six-foot Englishman must creep in at the front door, and then he can hardly stand upright—jostle one another along little lanes lined with cactus hedges that are overrun with creepers. So far this experimental village is not a great success. It is not certain that there is enough cultivable land to support the population; at present the villagers are mostly in debt. A few of the clever cultivators squeeze their neighbours and make good profits. But the school is a centre of hope; for the teacher has had a modern training and is teaching by the "project" method. I had seen several other village schools, where most of the children seemed to have only the vaguest idea of what they were learning. In one of these schools an unfortunate child was asked to point on the map of India to the Eastern Ghats. After some hesitation he dragged the pointer vaguely across the Arabian Sea. Poor child!

He is never likely to go farther than the sacred Narbudda river or the Vindhya mountains. The Eastern Ghats mean less to him than the Alps or the Pyrenees mean to a village schoolboy in Worcestershire.

At Makoriya they begin with things they know. The children had made a cunning plan of the village with little bits of coloured cardboard to represent the houses and "public buildings"—various colours for the different communities. They were really intelligent about this plan: not only did they answer questions about it correctly; they seemed to like explaining it. I think as these children grow up they will influence their parents, opening their minds to the need for subsidiary crops and village industries, perhaps even inducing them to see the merits of agricultural cooperation. Their influence should be like that of the Scout troops I saw in the refugee villages near Salonika. I believe the only way to change the minds of village people is through their children.

The "project method" seems to be a return to the methods of the old indigenous village schools. If it could be adopted all over India it might restore Indian prosperity within a couple of generations.

During the afternoon at Makoriya I had to show myself to the assembled villagers. They must be quite accustomed to English visitors; but they gazed as if they thought I was a white magician who, if I would, could rescue them out of all their distresses. But perhaps they were only regarding me—as I regarded the aboriginals—as a curious anthropological specimen.

Makoriya is three or four miles from a railway; the village horse was ill, so we were met at the station in the morning by an ox-cart. I was glad to find that R. G. was prepared to walk in spite of the damp heat. Our Indian companion, a teacher from Hoshangabad, walked a little way with us, but he seemed to think walking in such heat rather foolish, and he soon got into the ox-wagon. When I was in Bulgaria one of the Bulgarians I met said that the way to tell where the west ends and the east begins is by observing whether men wear their shirts inside or outside their trousers. This is an ingenious definition; for the

Bulgarians wear the shirt inside, the Rumanians outside. Of course, it is really a question not of east and west, but of north and south—in fact, of temperature. On our hot walk over the fields to Makoriya R. G. demonstrated to me the comparative coolness and comfort of wearing the shirt outside. No doubt it is cooler still to wear no shirt at all; and most Indians in the villages wisely prefer comfort to the artificial standards of civilization. Walking in the damp heat of an Indian October seemed to me quite a good form of exercise. We returned on foot, too. It is rarely possible for an Englishman to get such walks in this country. In the full heat of midday I walked in the jungle with the Indian schoolmaster; there we found great bouts of shade from the huge banyan-trees.

With G. W. M. I visited Bhopal and Sehore. This meant a journey across the broad and most sacred Narbudda river, then up through the hilly jungle that separates Bhopal State from the Central Provinces. At Sehore we were kindly entertained by the British Resident in a spacious hundred-year-old bungalow, with a beautiful garden sloping to the clear, silent river, where I watched steel-blue wire-tailed swallows hawking over the water. Over a bridge we came to the little church, just like a country church overhung with great elms (only, of course, they were not elms) in a forgotten corner of England.

In Sehore an Indian police official kindly took us to see the local opium shop, where he and G. W. M. cross-questioned the vendor. While we were there a young, ash-covered, practically naked *sadhu* came for some *charas,* a very potent drug made from hemp. Its use is prohibited in the Central Provinces. He and three other *sadhus* were sitting under a big tree near, and we went—followed by a large crowd—and watched them have their smoke. Each man in turn had the pipe, and took as long a pull as he could, having first uttered a loud "grace before meals," chiefly, I think, for our benefit. G. W. M. asked them how much they smoked at one time. "As much as God gives," was the reply; and apparently they consider that by smoking they get into a dreamy ecstasy in which they can better apprehend God. G.W.M.

commented in English that it seemed strange to suppose that God wished them thus to destroy their God-given bodies. No wonder people are apt (in India as elsewhere) to turn from such "religion" in disgust. The vast army of worthless *sadhus* (one in a hundred may be a saint), who live by terrorizing the people by threats of Divine wrath into giving them food and money, seems to be one of the major curses of India.

At Itarsi I got my first impressions of the conflict of religions. They are having a bad time at present with an Arya-Samaj lecturer. It is only a few weeks since Hindus and Muslims were killing each other at Nagpur, and this particular man seems to be "inciting to violence" in Itarsi. He is giving lectures in which he attempts to prove that Christ never lived. What value such lectures can be expected to have among the half-educated population of a growing railway junction like Itarsi it is hard to guess. They stir up bad blood; they certainly do not make for better religion—Hindu or any other. He invites the missionaries to his lectures and challenges them to answer him. G. W. M.—very wisely, I think—confines himself to statements of his Christian convictions, without attempting to argue. At one meeting apparently some of the local "Christians," who have repudiated all Church authority and are notorious for immorality, came armed with sticks. Next morning some leading Muslims came to G.W.M. to ask his co-operation in a counter meeting, but he refused.

I spent a week-end at Sohagpur, and there for the first time I came right up against Indian nationalism. This was just what I wanted, and the experience proved even more exciting than I had expected. R. D. P. kindly invited the local dignitaries to come and meet me on Sunday afternoon at tea. A number came, including officials, and pleaders, and others—mostly Hindus, a few Muslims. A high-caste pleader, who did not strike me as the outstanding personality, was the chief speaker. The others rarely intervened, but apparently they agreed with what he said. We started by discussing the Government's opium policy. I have heard strong attacks on the Government of India for its opium policy since I was a child—and I have read some of the things recently written by Americans. But I have never heard anything quite so violent as the attack of this Indian pleader. Every step taken by Government, whether good or bad, was put down to evil motives. He knew the subject well. Then we got on to other things, and always it was the same story. All the works of the British *Raj* were evil. He knew, of course, that I had never been in India before; so I suppose most Britishers out here would say that he thought he could make me believe any nonsense. I do not think that was his attitude. He seemed half-afraid to speak as he did; all the time he was screwing up his courage to speak out boldly, defiantly. Here was an Englishman to whom he dared to speak freely, pouring out all his passionate indignation, without being interrupted. I could not accept many of the things he said; but that was no reason for refusing to listen. Indeed, I came to India to use my eyes and ears rather than my voice; and here I was listening to something "authentic". I found him charming, friendly, misguided, illogical, irresponsible. Probably I shall meet many of his kind. I have listened before now to a Korean letting loose—or, rather, trying to control—his passionate indignation in the presence of a Japanese; I have heard Germans, in the presence of French, pouring out their wrath about the invasion of the Ruhr. It was not for me to show impatience in the face of this indictment of my country.

I doubt if all the others went quite as far as their spokesman. Perhaps they did not quite agree with him that the Government could only be moved by armed insurrection. But even the sub-judge, who seemed to me to be one of the most reasonable men present, said fiercely that the British officials have instructions not to mix with Indians and are perfectly ignorant of the real life of India: the missionaries know, he said, because they mix with people, but the officials know nothing and understand nothing.

After an hour's talk we had tea. Some ate fruit by themselves, but quite a few caste Hindus sat at table drinking tea with us. The high-caste pleader poured out our tea, but finally only ate fruit himself—though I think he was in two minds about it. Perhaps he felt that it would hardly do to compromise his caste after such uncompromising talk. After tea R. D. P. joined us; and he challenged them on some of the chief criticisms of Hindu social customs in Miss Mayo's *Mother India.* They did not give very clear answers; some things they admitted. The whole discussion was quite friendly.

It is noteworthy, by the way, that Miss A., at Sohagpur, who has intimate daily touch with Indian women, chiefly widows, has spoken to me more strongly than anyone in indignation against Miss Mayo's book.

As I have just given my first impressions of the Indian nationalist mind, I will write something of the conversation I had with H. on the boat between Port Said and Bombay. It was a great stroke of luck for me that I happened to come on the same boat as the one man I know in the Indian Civil Service with whom I could talk with complete freedom. I do not always agree with H., but I always respect his opinions.

He is no slave of conventional thought; but I should not expect him to get on well with Indians, or at any rate to appreciate their peculiar qualities. He has a critical mind and I found his criticisms very stimulating. Like most English administrators he obviously finds Indian "inefficiency" very difficult to tolerate; still more the absence of any "team spirit," or subordination of personal interest to public need. He has no use for Indian religion, or for Indian philosophy. In his heart I think he shares Macaulay's opinion of Indian culture, and he thinks most Indian thought is mere idle speculation such as undergraduates like to indulge in. On the other hand, he is no less critical of the British in India. He detests their perpetual games and foolish conventions. He thinks it would be a good thing if the British in India were honest Christians instead of pagan sportsmen, though he is no religious "conformist" himself; and he thinks the British Government would get on much better in India if it really governed instead of refusing ever to do anything that may offend some susceptibility or other. He thinks the ordinary Indian villager wants a good, just "father";

and that he has little chance of finding any among his educated fellow-countrymen.

Some hours of this sort of thing, together with exposition of India's economic problems, all expounded with a gentle and broad-minded tolerance, provided the innocent Westerner with a strong defence against the bewitching charm by which, as we all know, the East induces the Western traveller to see black as white and dross as pure gold. And what with books by Chirol and Ronaldshay, and other enlightened but critical Englishmen, I am surely sufficiently fortified.

II

CAWNPORE,
November 2, 1927

At Nagpur J. S. H. arranged a full programme for me, as I knew he would, though I had told him not to. Indeed, it was rather like a "League of Nations week". I spoke to the students of Hislop College and to a group of students at the Government College, addressed a public meeting and gave two lectures at the Philosophical Society, and took part in two college debates—one at Nagpur, the other at Amraoti, the chief town in Berar, a hundred miles west of Nagpur—and all on the League.

It is no easy job to talk about the League in India. To the ordinary Indian the League is just a gilded pill—or perhaps it would be better to say a concealed drug; at the heart of it is the Imperialism of the Western Powers. So my task was to put the other side in a way that might appeal: pointing to occasions when the Great Powers had been checked or challenged through the League; telling of the good work of the Mandates Commission as an offset to the French war in Syria; suggesting that India's new labour legislation is the direct result of the Geneva Labour Conferences; and that India's separate membership in the League is a step towards the recognition of her national status. I had some good questions to answer: Did the League put peace before justice? Why did it spend most of its time discussing the affairs of Europe? What would be the League's attitude if there was a rebellion in India against England? They thought that was a case for Article 10: I pointed out that it was not unless they proposed to invade England! But, of course, I agreed with the general criticism that the League's arrangements for securing "international evolution without war" are at present inadequate.

Perhaps the debate at Amraoti was the most interesting of these events. It was an inter-collegiate debate, preceded in the afternoon by a cricket match between Hislop College and Amraoti College. The Indian principal of Amraoti, an Oxford graduate and a Christian, is a man of amazing energy and vitality, and had brought together a large audience. Numbers of students made the earlier speeches, including two women, one of whom made about the best speech of the evening. She had really troubled to read up about the League, and talked facts instead of "hot air". Then came the "distinguished visitors". After most of us had spoken a local lawyer, evidently a very popular man, rose to oppose the League. He made a very clever speech—as "realist" as any European cynic could wish for; full of clever raillery at the high pretensions and rotten performances of the League—its failure to disarm, to interfere in the Ruhr, to protect Greece against Italy or China against Britain, or the poor Syrians or Africans, in spite of the "sacred trust". He pointed to the contrast between increasing tariffs and the pious platitudes of the Economic Conference. He wasted no words, but had some sharp, pithy innuendos for each thing he mentioned. Part of the audience applauded violently. It was almost the last speech of the evening. I thought hardly anyone would withstand it. But in fact we had over 70 votes to 250 on the other side, and I found some votes had been turned pro-League by the clever anti-League speech. A good many had seen through it and were disgusted.

I did not want the students, or the man himself, to think that I bore him malice for his speech, so I found him out afterwards and had ten minutes' talk with him. Lots of students gathered round to listen, and his cynicism quite crumpled up before a few "idealistic" suggestions. I believe this is quite characteristic. Cynicism of that kind is only skin-deep in most Indians. This man seemed to me thoroughly unattractive; and yet his worldly "realism" fell away when I suggested that for us who were still young (everyone within earshot was still young except himself) it was a fine thing to have a chance of influencing the world so that the League might yet be the thing that Wilson planned; and that it was better to spend one's life straining—perhaps in vain—for the ideal, rather than to add to the excessive amount of cynicism from which the world already suffered. I do not know if I really made any impression, but I went to bed (at 12.30) in peace.

Next morning (Sunday) Jack and I had to get up at five to motor back. It was thrilling setting off in the dark and meeting the dawn. We met many oxcarts, the eyes of the oxen gleaming against our headlights, the drivers asleep.

At dawn we stopped by a river and ate some food. Half a dozen wagtails were flying about on the rocks below; presently they came up on to the wooden bridge and sang a most sweet matin song to us. This big, dark, Indian wagtail has a much richer, sweeter warble than the soft ditty our pied wagtail often sings to himself, though he is supposed to be the same species.

After we had driven a good way farther the engine began to develop the most awful knock; ten miles from home it was unsafe to go any farther.

The first place where we stopped to examine the engine was at the end of a village that was suffering from plague. All the houses in the middle of the village were deserted, and the people had moved out into temporary shelters. It seems a good way of checking the spread of infection. It made the plague real and horrible—indeed, most terrifying. I thought of that realistic description of Sennacherib's army, "when they arose in the morning, behold! they were all dead corpses"! The knock of the car refused to be remedied. So I spent two and a half hours in a sun-baked spot, trying to shelter the tyres with branches of trees, and watching birds and feeling very sleepy, while Jack trudged into Nagpur to fetch another car out.

One day we attended a meeting of a very select students' discussion group, where a senior student read a learned and interesting paper on the present state of civilization—a philosophical discourse. The discussion afterwards turned mainly on the question whether a vital religion was the essential feature of every great civilization. A man who had just returned from Cambridge was very scornful of this idea, which was the thesis of the original paper; but it seemed to me that the disputants had different ideas of what a "religion" was; and the young man from the West was contemptuous of Hindu (and other) superstitions and practices and rituals, not of the spiritual life. But it was refreshing to hear him defending material improvement before his fellow-countrymen.

Twenty miles north-east of Nagpur there runs a line of hills which is famous to-day for its manganese mines; the deposits are among the richest in the world. I went out to these hills twice. One afternoon we motored to the holy city of Ramtek, and Jack and I walked up the vast flight of steps to the temples on the summit of the hill. Some of the temples are only to be entered by faithful Hindus. We heathen could but peer in at the strange stone images. But no one could deny us the glory of the view over wooded hills. It is a comfort that nature knows nothing of class or creed or caste. As we were mounting the steps we passed a little hut with naked children standing outside. As we passed Jack heard one of them say to his mother in a tone of awe: "How *tall* they are!"

The other visit was to a manganese mine. It was undertaken as part of my opium investigation. The manager had told C. that he thought he could give me some information, so C. motored me out there one morning. However, it appeared that the drug-takers were addicted to *bhang,* a mild form of hemp, not opium. Some said that they take it three times a day; others that they would take it if the sahib would increase their wages.

I learnt some interesting things about the manganese mines and labour conditions. Owing to the competition of Russian manganese, supported by the Soviet Government, the directors in England are worried about their profits; last year they only made 100 per cent.

This mine has no underground workings. Men and women were carrying heavy loads on their heads up precipitous slopes; they work long hours at low wages. Many of them are indentured labourers from Orissa and other parts of the country. Some, I understood, had been working there for twelve years. They live in the most wretched hovels, comparable to the tub of Diogenes, but perhaps rather more picturesque—and more draughty. The company is now providing "model" dwellings: that is to say, square, rather high, single-room, back-to-back brick buildings in long rows, with no windows. The benighted workers prefer their thatched hovels four feet high, overrun with creepers. I could not help sympathizing with them; though their huts must be flooded whenever it rains, and like ovens in hot weather. A school is also being built; it may or may not be used. The people do not want it, so the manager said, and the directors do not want the people to be educated, for then they will all want to be clerks. Still, a school looks well.

At one moment a woman came and threw herself on the ground and kissed all our feet; she then besought the manager to let her leave off work early, so that she might get home, two and a half miles away, before dark. In one of the "villages" the people came to ask the manager to come and see a man who was lying at the point of death. He warned us to keep back as it might be cholera; he himself went straight to the man and examined him. When he came back I asked what was the matter. "Oh, probably drunk last night", he said, making light of his own risk. It cannot be easy to keep discipline in such a place and yet to be a father to the people. I think this man is doing it.

I pursued my opium inquiries with some success at Nagpur. An Indian doctor took me among the depressed classes in the town and to an opium shop, and afterwards to a village inhabited by mill-workers. We found rather less baby-doping than he had expected. Things are improving under the influence of doctors, hospitals, Y.M.C.A. welfare work, etc. One oldish woman argued with the doctor that doping was necessary, because otherwise the children cried and wasted away; and the mothers of that region all produced doped babies. But other mothers managed better by various means. Finally the doctor took me over one of the Empress Mills. They are among the best cotton mills in India; and they have a model village, but I did not get there. Not being accustomed to mills, I was chiefly impressed by the roar of the machinery. There were plenty of women at work.

I called on the Excise Commissioner for the Central Provinces, and he poured out facts and figures about opium much faster than I could take them in. However, he also lent me the excise report where I could find it all, and this I have studied at leisure.

I must say I think the Provincial Government has done about all that a Government can do; it may be true that greater restrictions would only lead to more smuggling, and that there is little or no local anti-opium feeling. Education and propaganda by social workers and medical people seem to be the possible means of ending the trouble. The price has been so much increased that in the Central Provinces consumption is only one-third of what it was, and revenue only half.

Of course, at first revenue goes up with the increase of price. Continuance in price-raising after the revenue begins to fall is the real test of Government sincerity. The Central Provinces stand the test; Bombay does not.

From Nagpur I went to Poona, meeting J.W. G. on the way. First we had a week-end at the Christian Students' camp, a few miles out among the hills, overlooking a big reservoir. At the camp we ate Indian food and tried to sit on our legs. After half an hour in that position I found my joints—hips, knees, and ankles—terribly stiff. K. put me on to lead a small group of six or seven—there were only just over twenty altogether—each morning on "Christian Fundamentals", first about God and then about Christ. I wondered what they would make of my views. Of course, I went about it as gently as possible, but one has to be honest. One or two found me rather upsetting and disturbing. But several others seemed anxious to draw me on miracles and other difficulties; and the camp secretary, who was in my group, told me that most of them are brought up to accept certain dogmas which the missionaries treat as Christian foundations, not to be questioned, and they hardly ever meet a Christian who is prepared to discuss these things freely. Some of them said very sharp things about missionaries, complaining of their aloofness, their standard of life, and their dominating ways. But K. said the criticisms were milder than they used to be.

The position of these second-generation young Christians is very difficult, I think. They are outcaste from Hinduism, belonging to the Christian community in some cases from necessity rather than conviction.

There is great danger of their forming a separate and antagonistic community. One feels that in India, where communalism is such a curse, church membership may be a great evil. What is really wanted is people who can live as Christians, without having to belong to a separate Christian community. But I believe some Indians have lately tried to do this and it has proved a failure. I hope they will go on trying. It was encouraging to hear one of the students say that in their college life, at least, they get on all right with their fellow students if they show keenness or proficiency in work or games or something. The barriers are not insuperable. These students came from all up and down the west coast—from Baroda and Gujerat in the north, and from Mysore in the south.

Poona is a great place. No one who has seen the work going on there, growing at a tremendous pace, and spreading from there to other parts of the country, could ever again accept the easy British generalization that Indians are ineffective people who do not get things done. The Servants of India Society, started in 1905 by Gokhale, is a noble institution. It has under thirty active members. They are really members of a brotherhood (but they can be, and usually are, married, with families).

They have all consecrated their lives to true national service—not the brand to which the militarists give that name. The members "frankly accept the British connection as ordained, in the inscrutable dispensation of Providence, for India's good. Self-government within the Empire for their country and a higher life generally for their countrymen is their goal. This goal, they recognize, cannot be attained without years of earnest and patient effort and sacrifices worthy of the cause.... One essential condition of success in this work is that a sufficient number of our countrymen must now come forward to devote themselves to the cause in the spirit in which religious work is undertaken. Public life must be spiritualized." Many have offered, but few have passed the rigid tests required for full membership. This involves five or six years of strenuous training, and every member must promise always to put the country first in his thoughts, to seek no personal advantage for himself, to regard all Indians as brothers, to quarrel with none, to lead a pure, personal life. My impression is that they live up to their promises. Their funds are raised by begging; and since they threw themselves into the Labour movement many of the rich men of Bombay have refused to support them. They have often come under the suspicion of the authorities. They agree to live on a small salary, and they go all over India to meet the urgent claims of flood or famine relief, or other emergency work; they devote themselves to social service in many ways, including research, publications, and so forth. Those I met were greatly interested to hear of the Birmingham Social Diploma, and of all our work at Woodbrooke. They hope to introduce social service courses in the Indian universities.

Then there is the Seva Sadan Society, founded in 1910, a place where numbers of women get social training to fit them not only to be better housewives and mothers, but, still more, through teaching and nursing, to help their less fortunate fellow-women all over the country. A few miles out is an institution, founded thirty years ago, for Indian widows, to give them some education, and so make life more tolerable for them. This has developed until it is now the chief part of a Women's University, which was founded only three or four years ago. All this work was initiated by Indians, has been financed by Indians, and is run by them. The Widows' Institution has grown enormously; it has a religious basis, with a morning devotional meeting, which, one of the "Brothers" assured me, sets the tone to the whole life of the place.

I also visited Fergusson College, another great educational institution that is Indian in conception and management. It impressed me rather less because of some mangy stuffed beasts and dilapidated butterflies in the Biology Department. I suppose that may not have given me a true view of the place. Owing to the Divali holiday all these places were nearly empty of students, so I could not see the actual work.

One of my hosts at the Servants of India Home took me to see a wonderful Sanskrit Library, founded in memory of a distinguished scholar, Bhandarkar. I saw ancient Sanskrit manuscripts on palm-leaves from South India and on birch-bark from Kashmir.

One thing that impressed me about the Servants of India was the breadth of their interests. They "drew" me one evening on my European journey of this summer, and they knew a great deal about Balkan and Central European affairs. They asked me to suggest periodicals (in English) for studying European politics, and I found they had already got every one of those I mentioned.

After Poona I spent another day and a half in Bombay, and there I met Mr. Natarajan, editor of the Indian *Daily Mail*—a *very* different paper from the London *Daily Mail*—and of the *Indian Social Reformer,* an important weekly. He is an exceptionally able man. He dislikes nationalism because it may bar the way to internationalism. But he thinks the British have no longer any sense of mission towards India, and they have therefore forfeited the right to govern the country. Their refusal to accept the latest proposal to raise the marriage age is, to him, conclusive evidence that they are out of touch with national sentiment, which, he insists, has really changed about this in the last thirty years; and he believes that a self-governing India, in spite of all its difficulties, would now move more rapidly in the way of social advance than a British-governed India. All that I have so far seen and heard goes to support the view that the great majority of British officials out here now (with notable exceptions) have no ideal for India; they are the slaves of a thing called Efficiency, which means doing your work properly—no doubt an excellent quality not very common in India. But if you ask "Efficiency for what?" there is no answer; and I fear there is to-day as great a gulf—if not greater—between British officials and Indians than there has ever been: complete lack of sympathy. One of the "notable exceptions" told us a significant story. This man, a Bombay education official, had been to a conference of secondary-school teachers in the south of the Presidency. The teachers he had been meeting were mostly men who had had no proper training, and were perfectly innocent of modern teaching methods. They had lapped up all that he had to say with the greatest gusto, but what had impressed them most was a final address he gave on the "Spiritual Basis of Education". They told him that they did not think any Government official admitted that there was such a thing!

I left Bombay on the evening of October 22nd. At 5 a.m. next morning I noticed Baroda station, and soon after daylight we reached Ahmedabad and changed on to a metre-gauge line.

Rajputana certainly looked different from any part of British India I had seen. For a time near Mount Abu we were passing between fine wooded mountains, rising to over five thousand feet. We were not very far from the desert of Sind; there was plenty of scrub in most places, but hardly any cultivation. "Where the country was cultivated there were lordly wild peacocks, sacred birds in those parts, strutting about and devouring the grain. Monkeys also became more abundant, and in some places there were lots of deer. These are the things one sees. State corruption, opium addiction, and other such vices one can only infer from what people say, or perhaps from the fact that a great many people carry long sticks with ugly-looking knobs on the end—one might call them shillelaghs perhaps. I believe, in fact, the various States have very different standards, depending partly on the nature of the ruler. They are all under personal rule. The tendency in the more progessive, e.g. Jaipur, is to introduce officials and impersonal rule; and this is not altogether appreciated by the people, who have been in the habit of appealing direct to their ruler. Now they can only see cold officials who ignore their appeals. A slight incident in Jaipur recently led to a five-day "general strike"—really a popular protest against the progressive policy of the present ruler.

Jaipur is a fine city, laid out in broad, straight streets, all at right-angles, by a notable architect of two hundred years ago. Jai Singh, the ruler of the time, seems to have emulated his Mogul overlords, and built himself a fine palace up in the hills which I visited; but the town grew so fast that there was not room for it, so he migrated down to Jaipur, and had this new city laid out with a new palace. The hill-city, Amber, has many ruined and deserted buildings, including several beautiful Jain temples. The palace grounds at Jaipur contain a marvellous astronomical observatory, with many instruments to show the movements of the heavenly bodies. The instruments were recently tested and, I believe, found to be very accurate, though requiring slight adjustments owing to the passage of time.

I also visited a pass in the hills just above the city, where there are several famous temples and a perpetual spring that provides good bathing-pools for pilgrims. This perpetual spring is marvellous, as the rainfall at Jaipur is under twenty inches in the year. When I was there the mornings were delightfully cool, and the sun intensely hot most of the day. I believe sometimes the sun heat is 100° F. above the minimum night temperature.

My next stop was at Agra, where I stayed with an Indian, Pundit Kunzru, a Theosophist and a frank Liberal in politics (that does not mean a moderate necessarily; in his case it signifies an ardent Radical and Nationalist). I spent most of my three days unashamedly sightseeing: Agra Fort and the Taj Mahal one morning; the ruined city of Fatehpur Sikri, with its unruined palaces, the next morning; and the tomb of Akbar on the third day. I cannot give any useful impressions of these great Mogul monuments. The only comment of a personal kind I can make is, I suppose, proof that I have no proper aesthetic appreciation. For all the time I was seeing them, and observing the vast labour and priceless treasures that had gone into them, I could not get away from the oppressive sense that it was all wasteful vanity. The Taj is a tomb in which Shajahan and his favourite wife are buried; Sikundra is just a great tomb for Akbar; Fatehpur Sikri is his ruined city. I believe he himself had to desert it because the water was so bad. I could not even discover the name of the architect whose genius created the Taj. Pundit Kunzru's son assured me that there were many architects, and he went on to give numbers and figures of various kinds that I did not try to remember. Most of these buildings, like the pyramids, tell of nothing but the vanity of great tyrants—whose empires are as Nineveh and Tyre. The Acropolis, though I fear it was built by slave labour, helps one to appreciate the genius of the Athenian people—their religion and their view of life. The cathedrals of Europe are a monument to the spirit of the Middle Ages; and they still provide an atmosphere, as it was intended they should, where men in some degree get release from selfishness and materialism. No doubt the sight of the Taj fills men with lofty sensations, and the Pyramids may inspire awe. But it is hard to escape from the feeling that their purpose is to exalt and to "immortalize" men whose deeds are not worthy to be remembered. I suppose I must except Akbar from the useless tyrants: in his later life he made atonement for his early deeds of violence.

An Indian chaffed me that the British were leaving nothing in India comparable to the Taj. No, but if we leave a nation that has learned to free itself from age-old vices and to cultivate a sane mind in a healthy body it will be a far better memorial.

The last evening, just before I left, my host took me to see the Taj again after dark. Unfortunately the moon was only about four days old, so I did not get the effect of the Taj by moonlight. But the four minarets no longer looked, in the darkness, like lighthouses; and the dome looked even more wonderfully white and ethereal than by day.

Night travelling in India has advantages and disadvantages. I had a fair dose of the latter on my way from Agra to Cawnpore. I chose the best train, and it takes five hours or less—9.15 p.m. to 1.50 a.m. It was Saturday night, all the world was travelling, and I could only find space to spread my bedding on the floor of a second class compartment—already it had six occupants instead of five. A week before, when I reached Jaipur at 1 a.m., I slept comfortably in the waiting-room for four hours; at Cawnpore the waiting-room was horribly stuffy and the station outside noisy. By 6.15 I was longing for home comforts and *chota-hazri,* and I got both at the American Presbyterian Mission at seven.

On Sunday afternoon I went out to watch birds with three of the S.P.G. ladies. When we returned they decided their dresses were too dirty for attending the church service. They dropped me at the church door, but my courage quite failed me. I knew *I* had all the wrong clothes on, too; and my fellow country-men in India (particularly the respectable—official—Anglican type) alarm me dreadfully. So I had a quiet walk home to the friendly American Presbyterian Mission in the dark, and there I found the English mail, a weekly event which is always far more uplifting in India than any religious service could be. It is amazing how starved one gets each week and how exciting the prospect of the mail is. I am writing now on Friday at Delhi. The mail will have reached Bombay this morning. When can it get here? Tomorrow evening, or not till Sunday? Thus one speculates.

My older host was very kind in finding out the best people to give me opium information in Cawnpore. When he discovered that the Cawnpore opium consumption (or at least sale) was over ten times the League of Nations index figure, he was quite indignant with himself and his fellow missionaries that they had not known this before and done something about it. Two Indian officials between them gave me fuller insight into the drug habits of the people than I had got from anyone hitherto. One of them had had experience in many other parts of the United Provinces, too; so what he told me was specially valuable: Opium-smoking is still legal in the United Provinces, and there are still a few dens in Cawnpore and one or two other cities; but these dens are now illegal (under an Act of 1925). It is difficult, however, to find evidence to support prosecutions of offenders. This brings one up against the whole problem of law enforcement in India. I have been reading a remarkable book by Miss Carmichael, called *Raj: Brigand Chief,* about a dacoit in South India who became a Christian. I read it because H. told me he believed Miss Carmichael had been completely deceived by the man. So I began to read the book very critically, expecting the authoress to be emotional and unreliable. But the story is very convincing; and Howard Somervell evidently satisfied himself of its authenticity before writing the Foreword. Anyhow, the light that book throws on the methods of the police—false accusations, bribery, and most hideous torture—are enough to give one a horror of any police process in this country. I must add that Miss Carmichael, unintentionally, I think, brings out the responsibility of British Police officials for allowing these things to continue.

I would rather there should be hundreds of opium dens in Cawnpore than that they should be suppressed by such police methods. People I have talked to differ in their opinions about the police torture; but the false accusations and corruption are generally recognized. Of course, the ordinary point of view is that, in law courts in India, witnesses can be bribed to say anything, because there is no moral compulsion towards truthfulness. I suspect that this is an oversimplification. Perhaps if the law more nearly expressed the popular morality the people would do more to support its proper execution. And in my view that is what law always ought to do: it should never, I think, be very far ahead of popular sentiment. In India I am afraid much of the law is alien. A worse law, if better respected, might be better for the country. Perhaps this contradicts what I have just said about the failure to purify police methods!

The American Mission House where I stayed is at the north end of the town in the district of leather, wool, and cotton mills; and it is just opposite the "MacRobert Ganj" (settlement), belonging to the mills of a certain Sir Alexander MacRobert, benevolent autocrat, deceased. The younger of my hosts was formerly visitor at the *ganj*, and he took me over it one morning. It is not to be compared with Bournville exactly, but some of the houses have two large rooms, besides various offices and a courtyard. These are the better houses. Most have only one room with a courtyard. Miss Kelman, in *Labour in India*, quotes an American missionary, Mr. W. H. Wiser, as saying that "90 percent of the families living in one-room houses, with an open courtyard in front, at Cawnpore, had tried to create privacy for themselves by putting up screens of gunny cloth or bamboo, or reed or, mud walls"; and he urges that the mill-owners ought to do at least this for the workers. In the MacRobert *Ganj* they have now done it. There are brick walls almost everywhere hiding the front yard. Mr. L. pointed this out to me as a new feature. He said the rent had been slightly increased as a consequence. Attached to the settlement were two excellent schools—one for girls and infants, and the other for boys—and a dispensary. As often on this journey, the "distinguished visitor" had to write his name in the visitors' book with comments. I have committed myself to high praise of many Indian schools: but, after all, *every* school in India to-day deserves to be encouraged.

I was taken over the Agricultural College at Cawnpore by the student I met at Bhopal. It is for the United Provinces only (this youth's father comes from the United Provinces). It has very fine buildings, and I met several of the staff, who explained some of their work to me. For two years the students seem to do a fairly ordinary physics and chemistry course, with some botany; third- and fourth-year students do more advanced work. One man was expounding plant diseases (and showed me some specimens) to a class of senior students; but that was the only advanced work I saw. They have a garden where they dig the soil and grow flowers and palm-trees, and other apparently non-agricultural things. But I saw nothing to suggest experimental agricultural work, and I realized after I had left that I had seen no sign of any study of geology. In fact, the work at present falls a good deal below the standard of the buildings. But they have room to grow. There are 160 students.

One of the introductions T. gave me in Cawnpore was to Principal Diwan Chand, of the Dayanand Anglo-Vedic College, a remarkable educational effort of the Arya Samaj. What I have heard of the Arya Samaj hitherto had given me the idea of a body of violent religious bigots, responsible for stirring up communal strife. One of the bases is that "The Vedas are the books of all true knowledge". This is, I suppose, the basis of that passionate Hinduism which corresponds to the narrow Protestant Christianity that makes the same claim for the Bible. But people are often better than their creeds, and I think Diwan Chand will not be sending out 150 bigots into India each year.

I had a friendly talk with two of his students whom I met one evening when I was watching birds and the sunset by the Ganges; they certainly were not bigoted Hindu Nationalists. When I visited the Principal himself he, perhaps too easily, persuaded me to come and speak to his students the next day on "Whither the World is Tending"—the stupendous kind of question that Indians love to discuss. I tried to walk there and lost my way, and so kept them waiting nearly half an hour. That was a bad beginning, but they laughed when I said I understood that there was no such thing as time in the East, so I was evidently becoming Easternized. After I had spoken, the Principal expounded an interesting view of the three stages of society, or of civilization—dormant, aggressive, and contemplative (I think that pretty nearly expresses it). He thinks the Western nations are in the full tide of the second stage, and that the East is just emerging from the first into the second. In fact, he is a pessimist about the immediate future. Unhappily there was no time for discussion with the students; but I had some further talk with the Principal, and I found him ready to agree that there is in this age, as perhaps never before, the faint sound of what may be recognized as the voice of a world conscience.

The room was crowded with three to four hundred students. They have over six hundred. And the College is only eight years old, I believe. Buildings are going up all the time. The educational work of the Arya Samaj is remarkable.

One evening, when I was trying to get a peaceful walk by the Ganges, I came upon the famous *ghat* connected with that tragedy of the Mutiny. Perhaps that is one of the things we can try to forget. The place, like most Hindu sacred bathing-*ghats*, did not attract me. I think the average *sadhu* repels me more than any other Indian type. He seems to make the idea of religion disgusting. Most of them have a cruel, disdainful expression, quite unlike the friendly countenance of the ordinary Hindu.

Happily not all the bathing *sadhus* can spoil the beauty of the view across the Ganges, when the rosy sunset sky is reflected in its silently flowing waters.

III

IN THE ASSAM MAIL TRAIN,
CALCUTTA,
December 7, 1927

Now I have to record a week in Delhi, a few days at Benares and Ghazipur, a week at Santiniketan, and ten days at Calcutta.

I travelled from Cawnpore to Delhi on November 3rd, and enjoyed being able to take a long-distance journey by day. Most of the trains in India prefer to go secretly through the night. Luckily it was a cloudy day (drizzly when I left Cawnpore), so it was not too hot or too glaring. The country in the Ganges and Jumna valleys is perfectly flat, and in itself uninteresting; but there were marvellous numbers of birds, huge cranes, storks of several kinds, ibises, herons, flamingoes in one place, and quantities of smaller kinds.

My purpose in making this special journey to Delhi, which meant a rather serious break in my programme, was to get in touch with the Government officials, show myself to them (I presumptuously thought that when they had talked to me they would not cherish the idea that a dangerous revolutionary was prowling round the country), and find out what their opium policy was, and get all their latest publications. My mission was fairly successful. I had an introduction to Sir Basil Blackett, the Finance Minister, but he had just left for England; but Mr. N. M. Joshi had kindly given me an introduction to Sir B. N. Mitra, who is deputizing for Blackett. As I had few introductions of a less formal kind in Delhi, I went to a hotel, which perhaps helped me to cultivate the right outlook for dealing with the mighty ones of the earth. Most of the other inhabitants of the hotel were military men, some with their wives. I only talked to one of them, a pleasant little major, who sat at the same table with me, and evidently had had a good many years' experience of India. He seemed really interested in the country, and was very helpful in assisting me to see some of the interesting places in and around Delhi. He also told me that, in the Indian Army, when a man becomes an opium addict, it is very soon noticeable (he said "at once" not "very soon") and he is discharged as useless.

As to the officials, I had quite an amusing time with them. I telephoned to the Financial Secretary, explained what introductions I had, and went out by appointment and had a short talk with him. He told me that T. was the right man for me to see, and accordingly he arranged for me to see him the next day; and he also arranged for me to have a series of Excise reports dealing with opium, hemp drugs, alcohol, and so forth. These are a mine of information, but less illuminating than the Provincial Excise Reports, which I have been collecting together or consulting as I go from province to province. I find that in explaining my interest in opium I have to deal with three types of people, who are affected by various lines of approach. In explaining my position to Government people I have to talk about the League: as their chief aim is to prove that they are carrying out their obligations to the League, this affects them suitably. Christian missionaries of the normal type immediately begin to talk about Paton, and sometimes also of Dr. Datta. When I tell them I have been in touch with Paton and his writings and have read Dr. Datta's speeches, *they* are satisfied. Whereas with every Indian, from ancient Liberals and Government officials to ardent young Nationalists, the name of C. F. Andrews works like magic. The moment I explain that I am in close touch with him, their hearts are opened and their natural suspicions that I am another prying Miss Mayo are dismissed. But I have to be rather careful—among some missionaries particularly—to see whether I am to use the Paton or the Andrews opening. All this no doubt sounds very subtle and tortuous and double-faced; I expect it is; but it is quite necessary if I am to pursue my inquiries with any success. And all the openings are true in a measure, especially the League and C. F. Andrews.

I suppose I ought to say something about the New Delhi, now being built, where the British Indian Government works and the new Legislative Assembly debates. At first I thought it better than I had been led to expect; and I still think the Assembly Hall is quite a good building, But, taken all together, I think it is a poor affair, and a wicked waste of money. They could have cured all the bad flood areas of India, and built five thousand miles of metalled road in Assam (where I am now writing, after a motor journey of twenty miles on the main road—a road over which I should refuse to drive our Morris car) with the money. There is a tradition in India that when the rulers of the country have built their new Delhi they are overthrown; such traditions do not always work, but you never know. There is time for it to happen yet—time, and perhaps also cause.

The most amazing feature of Delhi is not its endless ruined monuments of forgotten empires, but its myriads of vultures and kites, feeding, I suppose, on the decay of the present time. Any day, at any time, if you look up into the air, you see them soaring low or high, in scores or in hundreds. Other Indian cities boast many kites and some vultures; but Delhi easily outdoes all the other cities I have visited.

So much for Delhi.

My journey to Benares by the Calcutta mail train was eventful. It was the night of the full-moon. Consequently I saw the Taj at Agra by moonlight after all; and even from a distance it looked very lovely. But at Agra the carriage was invaded by a large Muslim family, a father and two daughters (veiled) and two sons. There were already three of us in the carriage, and there is sleeping accommodation for five. They annexed one end of my bunk. If it had been in England I should have protested. As it was, with a great effort I tried to make the big man think that I liked sharing my bunk with him. I may remark that it is no pleasant job having to try to atone for the daily sins of 99 per cent. of one's fellow countrymen by such acute Christian meekness; and it was very acute. It gave me a chill (we had to have a window open, so I let it be the one that only affected me); and the chill was so acute that during a good deal of the next night as I lay in misery I really thought I had got cholera. My feelings towards the Muslim gentleman belied my words of the night before.

However, I struck some Christian fellow countrymen at Benares all right.

My two days in bed were well timed, for it poured with rain for three days on end. Everyone said it was "very phenomenal", or "rather unique", to have rain in November in the United Provinces, so I replied that the weather was always exceptional in every country in the world. We had a good fire each evening. By the time I was getting about again the rain was reduced to a November drizzle, and in that condition I saw the famous bathing-*ghats* and a number of temples at Benares. Only a few brave souls had the hardihood to come and wash their sins away that Tuesday morning.

I spent a delightful evening at the Hindu University at Benares. I had introductions to two of the young professors: one a Sikh, a political scientist; the other a local Hindu, a jurist, recently returned from England. The latter asked me to dinner, and the former came, too; my host's wife and sister were also at dinner, and one or two other guests, all Hindus; we had Indian food, but they had "compromised", and we sat round a table and had some utensils. The two men, who were great friends, had a vigorous political discussion. The jurist was more "left-wing" and sceptical about the effectiveness of democratic methods for achieving economic liberty; but political science had much the best of the argument. I am bound to say that I have so far met very few Indians who seem to me capable of what I should call sustained, exact reasoning. Their quickness of perception and imaginative qualities seem to get the better of them. But this Sikh professor was a notable exception. I should add that he had studied in London ten years ago under Graham Wallas, whom he obviously regarded as his master. Most of the other Indians I have met, who have shown that detachment of mind which is necessary for accurate thought, have been Government officials, whose whole outlook seemed Western, so that they have lost touch with the outlook of their own people. This man at Benares, and one or two of Tagore's young men at Santiniketan, seem to have learnt what was good from Western ways of thought without losing those fine qualities of intuition which are characteristic of Hindus.

Such a Hindu dinner party is regarded by several Englishmen of experience to whom I have spoken as still decidedly exceptional; and I must say that in all the Hindu homes where I have been since (except at Santiniketan), I have had my meals alone. But this is often because my hosts insist on supplying me with European food three or four times a day. It is not only caste. My impression is that caste is breaking down very rapidly indeed among the younger educated Hindus; and when the older generation (over fifty) are dead, it will largely disappear in all the centres of culture. Before the dinner I spent some time in the professors' common-room, and also called on the principal, a fine man, very tolerant.

At Ghazipur I stayed with another Wesleyan missionary and his wife. They were pleasant, quiet folk, with Quaker leanings. For instance, they had a silent grace before meals, so I was not in the hair-raising fear of being unexpectedly called on to "say grace", as in so many missionary households. Also my hostess was interested in the prevention of cruelty to animals. Assisted by a local Anglo-Indian lady vet., she was tending a pathetic-looking pony that had "strayed" in their compound with a ghastly sore. She knew the owner would turn up as soon as the animal was cured, but she hoped she would really give it a new life. It was lame and half-blind, but getting better every day and in every way. She was also getting signatures to a petition to prevent the water-buffaloes being used to drag heavy loads about the streets of Calcutta all day long. The water-buffalo cannot sweat, so it spends the heat of the day hippopotamus-like in the water—even in brown mud if nothing better is available. The unhappy beasts in Calcutta (I have seen scores of them since) are given no such chance, and the average length of their life is said to be one year.[1] In Calcutta one gets the impression that Western industrialism and commerce bring almost worse conditions for beasts than for men.

[1]This evil is now diminished.

Ghazipur is quite a small place, though once an important British military station; so that it has good roads, a number of large bungalows with pleasant gardens, and a large monument to Lord Cornwallis, who died there. The church, now Wesleyan, formerly belonged to a German mission. To-day the Government opium factory is the only "place of interest"; and it is more than half-closed. All the Government opium goes there to be passed through various processes, before being sent in a form suitable for eating to the provinces and to importing Governments; and some goes to Great Britain for manufacture into medicinal drugs. The control seems to be very strict and thorough at all points—at any rate, in the factory itself. There are elaborate cleaning-up processes each evening, and a cordon of police to inspect the workers as they go in and out; and the night-police who watch to see that no one comes in are themselves kept from the opium by cage fences. The manager, who showed me round, seemed to be a highly respectable elderly Anglo-Indian. I believe I saw all the processes, and he answered all the questions I asked; but I am never very good at thinking of the essential questions at the right moment; and I am much too inexperienced in business affairs to understand the significance of explanations of processes. However, I learnt a good deal about what happens to the nasty black glue that gives so much revenue to provincial Governments in India.

A night journey brought me to Calcutta, where I spent twenty-four hours before going to Santiniketan. I was two days later than I had intended, owing to my chill. As it happened, this turned out excellently, for C. F. Andrews had been back in Orissa for the flood relief work; and as a final outcome of a series of three telegrams that he sent (he corresponds mainly by telegram—a good practice in India, though I have not adopted it owing to my innate conservatism and tendency to foolish economies over trifles), he arrived, to breakfast with the S.s and myself at the Y.M.C.A. in Chowringhee on November 18th, and then straightway took me under his wing off to Bolpur, the station for Santiniketan.

We had under a hundred miles to go, but the train was almost incredibly slow; neither of us minded that, for C. F. A. says he finds he can get a little rest and peace and time for uninterrupted work in slow trains. Not that I gave him any chance of those things. But when you have met a man only once for an hour, and then corresponded with him for several years on a basis of mutual trust, you naturally want to find out what sort of man he really is; and I think we learnt a good deal about each other during those four or five hours. And he showed me all sorts of reports and appeals and documents about the miseries of large sections of humanity—in India, in South and East Africa, in British Guiana, and I forget where else.

After the deluge at Benares it was strange to come into a country less than two hundred miles away that was all parched and dry. The rains have failed so badly in the Bolpur region this year that it has been impossible to irrigate some of the rice-fields at all. At Santiniketan they spoke of a "four-anna crop"; that means only 25 per cent. of what it should be. That is nearly a famine crop. Bolpur is not the worst part. Floods in some places; famine in others: such is still the tale of India's annual sorrow. Starvation is now avoided as a result of British rule; but there is a great deal of semi-starvation and misery, and I cannot avoid the conviction that the floods at least are preventable, and would have been prevented long ago if we had been ruling India with a single eye to the benefit of the Indian people. But if I go into that I shall be in Orissa, which was a fortnight later. At present I must stick to Santiniketan.

Santiniketan means the abode of peace; and in the week I spent there I found great peace—rest, refreshment, and great encouragement. I was fortunate to come as C. F. Andrews's friend. That meant that all his particular friends on the staff, to say nothing of the students and children, adopted me without question; and the poet himself practically made me his personal guest.

Over sixty years ago Rabindranath Tagore's father, a man of religion, felt that the time had come for him to retire from the world and think upon eternity in some quiet hermitage. It is the custom for such a man to seek the hills; so to the hills he went, and wandered up and down, but found no place where his soul could be at rest. Then he turned to the rivers, but he found no rest by the rivers. One evening, as he was travelling in Bengal, he came to a great tree on an upland above the plains, in the midst of a stretch of open country, and there he halted for the night. As he sat under the tree and looked up at the sky he became possessed by a great ecstasy, which remained with him all through the night; and in the morning he said: "This must be the place of my *ashram.*" The great tree still stands there, and its fruit attracts glorious orioles and chattering mynahs and a lot of other birds. A stone seat has been erected near its base. Many more trees have been successfully planted near, in spite of the rebellious soil; each tree has some medicinal or other special value or significance. Surrounded by these trees, and secluded from the highway, stands the main building in which the poet started his school; and now many other buildings have grown, and are growing, on all sides. But the quietness and peace of the great spaces and the huge expanse of sky are not spoilt.

The school was started so that children might learn under the open sky, influenced unconsciously by the beauty of their surroundings, learning for the joy of learning, discovering themselves in music and art and the ancient culture of the land no less than in English and the three "r's" of the West.

Now there is also a college, which is recognized by Calcutta University. It, too, seems to be very liberal and humane, and the students do not live in terror of examinations. Latest of all, there is an agricultural school about two miles away, which is a centre of agricultural development in co-operation, rotation of crops, silkworm culture, and many other "agricultural accessories" for the surrounding districts, and a training-ground for young Indians from many parts of the country, who can and do carry back to their villages new ideas and new methods for making the debt-laden country more prosperous.

C. F. Andrews lives in a building at Santiniketan, some way from the central building and the school, and not far from the poet's house; rooms in it are reserved for unmarried professors. One was vacant, so I lived in it.

One of the first questions on arrival was as to my food. One Englishman, a learned Sanskrit scholar, Dr. Collins, had English food; or there was the Bengali students' mess, or the Gujerati students' mess. I asked what Mr. Andrews did. He messed, I was told, with the Gujerati students (their food is, on the whole, lighter and crisper, though rice is the staple article). So I said I would do the same. This was the right decision, for it meant that the students who looked up to C. F. Andrews adopted me, too. But in fact we only appeared at their mess half a dozen times. The poet professed himself scandalized that Mr. Andrews's unfortunate friend was made to sit on the floor and "starved" (as a matter of fact, I could never eat all the food they tried to give me)—to say nothing of eating with his fingers (I got fairly good at that). So he issued a standing invitation to breakfast (6 a.m.) and dinner (7.30 p.m.), and seemed to expect me to turn up at other meals, too. And what with invitations from other people, including the Bengali students and the boys in the school, meals were taken in many places. The meal with the small boys was a great occasion; they nearly forgot to eat with excitement at having Mr. Andrews and his funny English friend eating with them. And when we went on a tour of inspection of their dormitories and workshop—made by themselves, and in which they were turning all sorts of odds and ends into marvels—they adopted me as their *guru* without further ceremony.

I also worshipped with the boys once or twice. At about 6 a.m. they sit on the ground, rather scattered about, each on his own mat, for about fifteen minutes in silent meditation. I think they were about as much interested in the passing birds as I was; but I should guess that the silence does them a lot of good. If it helps to keep them gentle and restrained and kind in the face of provocation it will have done a good work and given them what they are likely to need.

Once a week everyone gathers in the temple. The girls sing one or two hymns and the poet gives an address.

I ought to describe the poet and his conversation. We generally had rather silent meals (that is, of course, the old Hindu custom, but Tagore does not stick to it as a principle). I had a sneaking idea that perhaps one reason of his friendliness to me was that I was not always trying to make him talk. But the right balance is not easy. For he likes being drawn when he is in the mood to talk. When he does speak he expects his audience to attend, and to pay the respect due to an oracle; and he could give a poet's justification for this. It seems that he never thinks before he speaks, even when giving an advertised lecture. What comes is what the moment and the occasion demand; and it is the subconscious mind that does the work. So the oracle is not his conscious mind, but his inner daemon. Lucky the man who, like Tennyson and Tagore, is blessed with a subconscious that does not always talk drivel! But I am sure every subconscious must sometimes dish up drivel, unless the conscious mind is on the alert to check it.

I cannot remember how one conversation developed, but after a time the poet launched into a denunciation of the British attitude in India that made a great impression on me. I ought to have written down some of the things he said immediately after. C. F. A. told me that when you listen to him you receive a deep impression, but afterwards you find the exact argument or words difficult to recall; and so it has proved. But I do know that he spoke quietly, gently, without passion, but with strong conviction, of the alien nature of the system of government, of its lack of imagination and insight, of the intolerable arrogance of every Englishman in the country, who takes it for granted that he is a privileged person, to be served by Indians as his inferiors; that this has developed a slave mentality; and having created a slave mentality, we then jeer at the people for their incapacity.

By this he does not mean, of course, that we have turned the Indian people into chattels. He is thinking of our intellectual attitude. We have told India that her philosophy, her religion, her way of life were foolish and childish; she must copy the English: they alone know the real secret of life. We have killed initiative. As for the present excuse for prolonging the agony, he is convinced that Hindus and Muhammadans can never learn to live together while a third party is holding them in leash. I told him of the Irishman who in pre-Free State days said, "If only the English would go away, and leave us to fight it out in peace among ourselves!"—which delighted him. The longer we insist on remaining in India the worse things will be in the end. He has no illusions about India's capacity for self-government. He thinks there will be a time, perhaps a long time, of chaos; and he does not think India will adopt democratic government, even in the end. But, however all those things may be, what he sees to-day is that the British have fulfilled their task, and are simply an obstacle to progress, stultifying the mind and soul of the people.

I had been hearing things of this nature from a good many other Indians; but I had hardly expected it from Tagore, the internationalist, the admirer of Western culture. Several other men came in while we were talking (or while he was talking), one of them an Indian magistrate. Tagore said to him: "We are talking sedition; you will have to arrest us." He answered: "I come here as a pupil, not as a magistrate." And it was clear that this was no mere polite speech. It was the true Indian attitude to the Gurudev, the great teacher.

At one point in our conversation I suggested that, after all, the English had perhaps done some good in India by introducing games, which promote physical health and devotion to the welfare of the "team". I asked him if he thought that was our chief contribution to the world. Immediately he seemed to realize that his denunciations might have hurt me (they did a little, for though I have had plenty of occasions for being ashamed of being English since I came to India, I care very much that England should have a fair name in the world; but I did not want to show him that I was hurt). So thereupon he began to show his appreciation of the West—of our literature especially, and of our great heroes of freedom. Our rule, he said, is in many ways better than that of other Western peoples in the East—American, Dutch, or French. We allow so much personal freedom.

And that, of course, always makes the contrast more bitter. It is largely the inspiration of England that has stirred in India the passion to be free, to call her soul her own, to develop her life, through struggle and disappointment perhaps, to her own appointed goal. And now the descendants of our heroes of freedom not seldom dismiss the efforts of India to follow in the same path with supercilious contempt. Many of us, who pretend to be followers of Christ, are scornful of India because her people are gentle and kind and forgiving, instead of being strong and ruthless.

I am not quite sure how much of this is Tagore and how much is my own, or else derived from other conversations with other Indians. I think it is rather like the Fourth Gospel!

At another time he asked me what I thought about modern English poetry. I had to confess that I read very little of it, but that I found most of it rather second rate, attractive but not abiding, exciting sometimes but not inspiring. He agreed. As to Masefield, he said he found him unreadable, because of all his slang, which only an Englishman can understand. Drinkwater he suspects of playing with passing emotions—nothing permanent. He had read some of Rupert Brooke's poems and found them good; and was interested to hear a little about him and his mother. He met him at Cambridge. His summary of the situation was this: "Shelley and Wordsworth and Keats and your other great poets had something definite that they had to say. They had to preach freedom. It may not have been the greatest message; but it was sufficiently great to create great poetry. To-day your poets have nothing particular to say, so they cannot write great poetry." I commended Gordon Bottomley to him. He had not read any of his poems; but I think his criticisms would still apply.

The poet's friendship for C. F. Andrews is charming. He is fond of upbraiding him gently for the sins of his countrymen at one moment, and a moment later he calls him a most dangerous firebrand, who brings discredit and suspicion upon his peaceful educational centre. C. F. A. is constantly going off to various parts of India—not to mention South or East Africa—on his mission for the poor people of India. He is called "The Friend of the Poor" in India. When he took leave of the poet to go to the Indian Trade Union Congress, Tagore asked him if he would ever come back again. "Yes," said Andrews, "after five days."

"Oh, five weeks," said Tagore. That is quite a fortnight ago, and I very much doubt if he has been back yet.

If you were to ask an Englishman in India what Indians are like in an emergency, I am afraid he would almost certainly say (with foolishly violent emphasis), "Hopeless—utterly useless". Even if it were universally true, it would not necessarily involve the condemnation which the Englishman seems to assume. But it is not. One day at Santiniketan the poet's son took me to see some of the villages where co-operative effort is leading to many improvements. We had just left one village when, looking across to Santiniketan, we were horrified to see a large column of smoke and a great flame rising up into the sky. Luckily I had my binoculars with me, and we could see that it was not an important building.

When we got back half an hour later we found the last embers were just being extinguished. The students, men and women, and the boys and girls, had promptly formed into three double rows from the three wells to the burning shed, and passed buckets along; at one well at least the girls were doing the actual hauling of the water. By wise generalship at the beginning the fire had just been kept from the servants' buildings, which, like the burnt shed, are thatched. None of the "excitable, unpractical" Indians was hurt, but one stolid Mongol servant burnt his hand.

By the way, the poet's son married a widow, with the poet's warm approval. But they had no children, so there were scornful comments from the orthodox. Then if happened that a poor woman at Santiniketan gave birth to a child and went out of her mind. The daughter-in-law looked after the child, and when the mother died adopted her. She is a jolly little girl.

I had excellent talks with a Parsee, Vakil by name, who is a professor of English literature. He was at Oxford, preparing for the Indian Civil Service, but he decided that he could not go into Government service, so he has given up all his prospects and is living very happily, married, and with two children, at Santiniketan. He is very anti-British; he said the Indians described by Forster in *A Passage to India* are typical of the kind who mix with British officials. They lose all their moral fibre and have to be deceitful. We argued about the possibility of avoiding another world war. He urged that the real economic jealousies of people in England and America, for example, are quite unaffected by League obligations and Parliaments and Foreign Offices. I argued that public opinion was becoming alive to that fact, and would soon insist on cutting the bankers' claws. He thought a war between the Anglo-Saxon Powers and Russia was almost inevitable; and he saw in it the hope of liberation for Asia—perhaps the only hope. I said I thought it would mean the ruin of civilization, including Asiatic civilization. He had an unusually Western mind—perhaps that was why he was so conscious of the crimes of the West—but withal he had the true modesty of the East; he was prepared to listen to my rather half-hearted defence of Christian missions even. And we found ourselves in almost complete agreement in religious views.

By the way, I had a very good talk one evening during a twilight walk with C. F. Andrews about Christianity and the other religions. His attitude is practically this, as I understand it. Let each religion be true to itself, respecting the others, and ready to learn from the others. A Christian living in that spirit is welcome anywhere among enlightened Indians.

It was a happy thing for me to be able to claim cousinship with Willie Pearson, whose memory is very green. Lately they made a new bit of road below the school, and called it Pearson Road. At the "dedication" C. F. A. pointed out that the road was very suitably aiming straight towards the Santal village, a little way off, whose people Pearson had tended. One of the schoolboys came to him after and said: "I have thought of a much better thing about the road than you said: Look where the sun is setting. The road leads from east to west, and from west to east, and that is what Mr. Pearson was always doing."

I did not go to any of the ordinary lessons or lectures, but I often saw the small groups of students sitting round their *guru* in the shade of the trees. I went over the Art School; and saw not only art treasures from various Eastern lands, and remarkable work done by one or two of the Tagore family, but also beautiful and expressive work on which some of the students were engaged. And I listened to a course of lectures by C. F. Andrews on "World Cultures"—a most informing summary of the great truths realized and expounded by the Buddha, the sages of China, and some of the seers of Western Asia and the Mediterranean. One hardly knew whether to be more cheered or depressed to think that the great truths of spiritual well-being, which we are still so slow to learn and practise, were proclaimed from end to end of Asia two thousand years ago. The depth of C. F. Andrews's own Christian conviction and experience shone through his exposition of the non-Christian systems. He seemed to insist that truth is truth, whatever title it may bear.

IV

Madras,
End of the Year

After my visit to Santiniketan I returned to Calcutta on November 25th, and remained there till December 7th, except for a short visit to Orissa.

In Calcutta I stayed at one of the Y.M.C.A. hostels. Here I mixed for the first time with the young English "commercials" of the country.

It is practically impossible for an Indian to have rooms at this hostel; there is a separate place for them. One, with a very light complexion, was there when I arrived, and I shared a double room with him. He never ventured to public meals (not for Hindu caste reasons), and apparently the prospect of sharing his room with an Englishman nearly scared him out of his wits. But F. S. had somehow convinced him that a Quaker would be all right. Actually I found him a most delightful companion. He was in the Imperial Bank of India—a most pleasant, open, reasonable man who has no use for his country's politicians, but wanted to see drastic social reforms in India, and believed it possible to achieve them under the present political regime. He told me that, whereas you would suppose from *Mother India* that nearly all Indian students had venereal disease, he had been at a residential college for four years, in residence with some four to five hundred students during that time, and he had only heard of two cases, though he thought most students in India were fairly open about such things.

When he found I was really going he decided that he could not face a possible race-prejudiced successor, so he found rooms elsewhere and left the Hostel. By good fortune I met him again with his father, when I was passing through Calcutta the day after Christmas, and his father invited me to their home at Allahabad.

My English fellow residents at the Y.M.C.A. Hostel at first filled me with depression. After a few days I found that they were, of course, quite good fellows, like anyone else, provided one kept within certain limits; but their attitude to politics and to the "native" was unspeakable—or rather the attitude of the more vocal of them. They were men in minor business jobs, who come out for a number of years, who are prohibited as part of their contract from marrying, who have not been educated to appreciate people of another race and outlook. One of them declared that he had never once met a Bengalee who could be trusted; all, everyone, was dishonest, and as incompetent as he was dishonest. Another had, so F. S. told me, risked his life to save an Indian who was drowning in the Euphrates during the war; but he declared he would never do such a foolish thing again. As a matter of fact, no doubt he would, if the occasion arose; but meanwhile he reviled the whole race. I think it is a great disaster from every point of view that such men are being sent in scores year by year to live this unnatural life in a country whose people they cannot understand; and who cannot understand them. I cannot see that any economic facts of to-day make it necessary. I am sure it does much to deepen the gulf between the two races.

While I was in Calcutta the St. Andrew's Day dinner, a great annual function, took place, and a leading business man made a speech which some of these men hailed as the last word in political wisdom. It was the speech of a man who, starting by denouncing the whole race of politicians as futile agitators, proceeds to make the worst possible kind of political speech, foretelling ruin because Indians are allowed to share in the government, and sighing for the "good old days" that never existed outside his imagination.

In the midst of these depressions I went to breakfast one morning with Dr. W., and had a delightful time with him. He was telling his wife and daughter that his servant was having a day off for some family function, and they seemed rather amused at the ease with which the man got days off. Dr. W. turned to me: "I have had this servant", he said, "for over thirty years. I can trust him with everything. He is just as safe as the Bank. He carries thousands of rupees for me sometimes, and he has never lost anything." In contrast to the kind of thing I had been hearing at the Y.M.C.A., this was like sweet music.

As Dr. W. was taking me round the laboratories, he rebuked one student because he was leaning over his work with his hands on the desk. "No wonder you fellows get hollow-chested," he said, "leaning over your work like that." The youth was obviously much ashamed to be so rebuked before a stranger. "Hollow-chested" is one of Miss Mayo's epithets for Calcutta students. I tried to rise to the occasion. "But," I said, "I think I have never seen so many upright people as in India. I suppose it is because they carry things on their heads." "Carry things on their heads!" exclaimed Dr. W.; "these fellows never do that! It would be good for them if they did." General good humour was restored ; and no doubt the rebuke which I dare say was intentionally made in front of a stranger, was not forgotten. All the same, I must say that I did *not* notice the students of Calcutta to be hollow-chested and round-shouldered. Indeed, I suspect that Miss Mayo was deceived by the fastening of the Indian *dhoty*, which is apt to give a dyspeptic, round-shouldered appearance to the most upright man. As to her "fly-blown Russian pamphlets", I could discover none in Calcutta; and it is most improbable that these should ever have been common. Anyhow, it has nothing to do with her case. If she had written "fly-blown pamphlets on sex", it would have been much nearer the truth, and much more nearly connected with the special subject of her investigations. But perhaps she remembered that pamphlets of that kind are to be found in Western cities, too; the difference in India is that they are much more openly advertised.

I find that some of the things Miss Mayo pretends to have seen at Kalighat could not have been seen by any Westerner; and some of the more disgusting things she records there as normal are so exceptional as to be practically unknown.

Of course, the real scandal of the first chapter is that Kalighat, far from being typical, as the reader might naturally suppose, is a very rare relic of the abominations of the past.

I gleaned a good deal of useful information about opium in Calcutta. One of my introductions was to the Rev. Herbert Anderson, a Baptist missionary who has done a great deal for temperance in Calcutta, and is now a member of the Licensing Board. He has also been serving lately on the local committee for investigating the causes of excessive opium addiction in Calcutta, and he showed me the mass of evidence collected and some statistical tables prepared from it. The report is likely to contain demands for drastic reforms. One afternoon he took me to several opium shops and to an opium-smoking den. The latter was in the Chinese quarter, but the great majority of opium-smokers in Calcutta are Indians, not Chinese. The majority of the opium-buyers at the shops struck me as of rather a low type, but they included men of all classes, some of them evidently of good position and refined appearance. There is no shame attaching to opium consumption. At a *ganja* shop, on the other hand *(ganja* is derived from hemp, like *bhang* and *charas),* we found the people reluctant to buy while we watched. *Ganja* is a pure intoxicant. The one man who was communicative at the *ganja* shop said he bought it because it made him "as strong as a tiger".

I also talked to Major Chopra, an Indian with a Cambridge M.D., in the Government Medical Service. He has been carrying out important inquiries as to the medical effects of opium and is publishing his results. Most of his inquiries so far have been among Sikhs in Calcutta and in the Punjab. The taxi-drivers in Calcutta are nearly all Sikhs and nearly all opium-eaters. They are furious drivers, but personally I found them safe. Major Chopra's conclusions are cautious, but in fact they undermine several of the common notions about opium in India.

The Bengal Commissioner of Excise, S. K. Raha, an Indian to whom Sir Atul Chatterjee had given me an introduction, invited me to see him at the Calcutta Club. This seems to be a good institution where Indians and British of the higher ranks of business and official life mix in quite a friendly way.

A member of the editorial staff of the *Statesman* joined us in our talk, and gained a good mark from me by quoting Lowes Dickinson's *Impressions of Travel* with approval, to the effect that, if Englishmen in India appreciated the real issues with which they are confronted, most of them would go home at once.

One Sunday evening, at my request, Nalin Ganguly and his pleasant young brother Alin took me to the Brahmo-Samaj meeting. Unfortunately the "minister" was an old-fashioned man, whose ideas about the length of a service and its conduct might have satisfied Dutch peasants. The service, with alternating prayer and chants and then a vast sermon, went on for over two hours with no silence. The only thing I understood was the text of the sermon from Paul, "Woe be unto me if I preach not the Gospel" (rather a surprising text for a "non-Christian"). It came three times over in the sermon, and the preacher evidently believed that Paul meant to add the words "at great length". All the same, in spite of some weariness of the flesh I was interested because of the audience. There was a good crowd, and although a certain number wisely retired before the sermon, the great majority stayed to the end, some sitting on the floor all the time. The preacher himself sat all the time on, rather than in, the pulpit. Men formed the great majority, and they were men of all ages. The old men especially looked just like old men who would relish one and a half hours of Wesleyanism in England: the same patriarchal appearance and kindly faces, even the very same features; others had curious faces, quite different from anything you would see in the West. When they began to get tired (I was glad a few showed *some* sign of this human failing) they gently swayed their bodies to and fro. One man, who looked quite harmless, joined in the final chant in a most alarming fashion. As the music rose and fell he joined in the high notes, usually out of tune, in a voice that ascended to an awful shriek and stuck there, while the music went quietly on.

As we were returning on a tram, an elderly man sitting by me, who had been at the service, asked me if I were a Unitarian. "No," I said, "a Quaker." Oh, yes, he had heard of them. Did we have services like the one we had just attended? "No," I said, perhaps a little violently; and the poor man seemed disappointed, so I explained our manner of worship, and I think he was interested—or at least mollified.

Can it have been this same Sunday (I think it was) that I spent the afternoon at Serampore? Having spent two nights in the train, and two very arduous days visiting Balasore and Cuttack (in Orissa), I was very tired and sleepy; it was a hot afternoon, I was given a heavy lunch, and my good host, a young Christian lately returned from England, was determined to show me all the sights in about three hours. I just managed to keep awake; but in the famous library, where the wonderful relics of Carey and Marshman are preserved, I *very* nearly fell asleep over the precious volumes. I saw various ancient Danish buildings—Serampore was the Danish trading place in pre-British days. I was taken to see the inside of some huge Hindu family mansions. The head of one of these inquired if I was another Miss Mayo, who was going to write a book about the wicked drug habits of the Indians. My host regarded this as a joke. I gather that he is always girding at his fellow citizens of Serampore for the rotten condition of their drainage, etc. (he very well may do), so I suppose they suspect him of introducing Westernizing Miss Mayos to see (and smell) the evils of their town. Happily we got a more friendly welcome at the next house where we called, although S. B. criticized this good man for tolerating a particularly odorous stagnant pool just opposite his front door; he was extremely friendly, gave me a most welcome cup of tea, presented me with his published works (a not uncommon habit in India, but this was a translation into English of an ancient Hindu myth, which I have much enjoyed reading), and escorted us to the railway station with many expressions of kindness and appreciation of the honour I had done him. On the way to the station we saw an enormous dead snake on the railway bank, the only snake I have seen in India, apart from those kept by snake-charmers.

Now I must say something about my visit to Balasore and Cuttack. I went there at the suggestion of C. F. Andrews. They belong to one of India's "black spots" of heavy opium addiction.

A special committee of inquiry has been appointed, consisting of two officials—one a reactionary and the other a man of good intentions, but reputed to be weak—and two non-officials: one a nonentity, the other the father of the chief opium-vender. I have a copy of the questionnaire, which is distinctly tendencious; and a doctor we visited, who read us his replies, had fallen into several of the traps set for the unwary. I was accompanied by an American Methodist Episcopal missionary from Calcutta, named B. W. Tucker, who has become very much like C. F. Andrews in outlook and activities, identifying himself with Indian life, a quiet, unassuming, level-headed man, whom I liked very much: not at all the aggressively anti-British type of American who does so much harm. We saw a good many people, including the afore mentioned enlightened official, with whom we had a frank and friendly discussion; I hope our visit may have helped to strengthen his resolution, but I doubt if it can have had much other effect, unless perhaps as an encouragement to a few of the nationalist leaders, who have a very difficult task. But they were about to have a far greater encouragement, in a visit of Mr. Gandhi, who has since been there to make a study of the "poverty problem of Orissa". Tucker was discussing plans for the visit while we were there, and he and Andrews both went to help carry it out.

For three days no one dared to approach Mr. Gandhi, except one decrepit and wretched untouchable, who was too far gone to fear the consequences. Whispers had gone round that it would go ill with any who laid their complaints before him, and the terror of the police made them fear even to approach one like Mr. Gandhi, whom they reverenced and loved.

The Ooriyas (the people of Orissa) are, indeed, a sorrowful people. They are very poor, so most of their country has been attached to the rich province of Bihar, while some are in the Central Provinces and some in Bengal. Many have to migrate to other places on labour contracts: I had seen them at the manganese mines near Nagpur; I was to meet the Ooriya problem again very soon in Assam. But their chief afflictions are at home—opium, extortionate rajahs, and floods. This year's flood has been specially bad: 80,000 people have lost their homes, a far larger number their crops. In the Indian States fifty-six people are known to have been drowned; probably an equal number were drowned in British territory. The number may have been a good deal higher. The destruction was considerably worse—so C. F. Andrews and others who had been on the spot told me—than in Gujerat, whose bad floods have been reported even in English papers. Yet the most helpful thing the local British official could do in this emergency was to assure the world that the first reports spread by the local people were "greatly exaggerated". The flood-affected area is on the main line from Calcutta to Madras, between Balasore and Cuttack; for some time the mail trains were delayed; but as all the passenger trains cross that section by night no European would see the floods. No special correspondents went out from Calcutta, as they did from Bombay to the Ahmedabad floods. I believe the only white men who had really been all about the flooded areas were C. F. Andrews, Tucker, a Salvation Army captain, and another American missionary whom we met at Balasore. When Andrews tried to raise relief funds in Calcutta he was met with the official statement that the early reports were exaggerated, and that the Government had the situation well in hand. For the Gujerat flood relief 216 *lakhs* of rupees were raised. This meant that bad villages, even if not totally destroyed, could be completely rebuilt. The disaster was turned into an opportunity for improving housing conditions.

In Orissa, on the other hand, only 9 *lakhs* were forthcoming. A British official insisted that it was important that the people should *not* be provided with better houses than they had had before. So the largest sum granted for rebuilding any one house was eight rupees. In Gujerat over 100,000 rupees were spent on one village of 150 houses. When the local official finally realized that something must be done, Andrews and the Congress people had already begun relief work. The official tried to persuade Andrews to desert the Congress people and administer a Government fund. No wonder Andrews refused to desert his friends! At Cuttack we had breakfast with the W.s. They had guests, a local education official and his wife and her sister. When I referred to the floods, this man immediately quoted his friend the local official, and talked about the pampered, whining people. I do not remember just what Tucker said, but he quietly and politely made it clear that he knew of the state of affairs at first hand and the other man did not.

I have not yet referred to the rajahs' part in this wretched state of affairs. There are a good many in those parts (not all bad, of course) with minor States under their control. The particular rajah who owns most of the flooded lands appears to be a specially poor specimen. He has shooting-parties for British officials, subscribes liberally to college endowments, and so forth; but he will tolerate no interference with his peasants.

It seems that one district has had floods eight years in succession. The first Government Commission to consider what could be done to prevent these floods was appointed, I believe, over eighty years ago. Many have been appointed since. A new one has been appointed now. Either they propose mild palliatives, which are almost useless; or they propose drastic action, which is turned down on the score of expense.

Andrews and Tucker, who have been constantly backwards and forwards to this region this year, both agree that the people are tragically feckless and wanting in leadership. Far from being pampered and loud in their complaints, they are neglected, crushed by their overlords, and they suffer in silence.

Of course, I am unlikely to have got quite a true picture in this very short visit; but I returned to Calcutta feeling more ashamed, more disgusted and sick with the present government of India, more angry and rebellious than I had ever been in my life. I think what I felt most was the callousness of those who should know better.

T. gave me introductions to two of the leading Swarajists in Calcutta—T. C. Goswami and J. M. Sen Gupta, the latter the Mayor of Calcutta. He was at Cambridge a little before my time. I called on him, and he invited me to dinner, when Mr. Goswami and the two delegates of the British Trade Union Congress were present, Purcell and Hallsworth. This was a disappointment, as Purcell talked all the time. My earlier talk with Sen Gupta was more interesting. He then assured me that, far from being extremist agitators who were misleading the youth of the country, he and his friends were having the utmost difficulty in persuading the young men to keep to the path of constitutional action: when violence occurs it is not because of their advice but in spite of it. All the same, he seemed to doubt whether the British Government would ever be roused to consider the demands of India seriously until violent outbreaks have taken place. He knows they can easily be crushed, but they may shake the stupid Englishman out of his complacency. (He did not use that rude expression.)

I am afraid there is some truth in this analysis, both of the Indian situation and the English character.

Once again we can see how poetic justice works. The Englishman constantly declares his belief that the East can understand nothing but force. The Easterner naturally comes to believe that this Western trust in force proves that the Westerner himself can understand no other argument. The vicious circle is complete. I cannot test Mr. Sen Gupta's assertion that he and other acknowledged leaders are trying to dissuade the students from violence. The ordinary European would brush it aside as nonsense—the clever pretence of a firebrand. For myself, I am inclined to think it is true. From what I have seen of Indian students I certainly think many of them want to use force. I do not think they are restrained by cowardice, but rather by ancient Hindu tradition, perhaps also by rather reluctant consent to Mr. Gandhi's principle of non-violence; and, it may be, by older men who have learned wisdom and caution through experience.

Before leaving Calcutta I want to record one impression that has been made upon me in India generally, but especially in Calcutta. It is the refinement of feature that is characteristic of a great proportion of Indians. Over and over again I have seen men wearing nothing but a loin-cloth doing heavy manual work, whose faces suggested intellectual distinction and spiritual refinement. When you meet people casually in the street it is quite impossible to judge of their education and social standing from their general appearance. Can it be that in the West I look at people's clothes and judge them by that; and here, where they hardly have any, one has a chance to see the man himself? Or is there a real difference, signifying that they have learnt the secret of escaping the degradation that so often in the West seems to accompany tasks that we count mean? I was speaking of these things to my father-in-law, and he told me that, according to Sir Francis Younghusband, you can travel from the Himalayas to Cape Comorin and never meet a vulgar person. I think there is much in that saying. The struggle for existence in India is terribly severe, and no doubt it leads to much cunning and brutality; but the lust for wealth as such would seem to be rare. "Spiritual values" are, perhaps, more generally recognized. A man may be a very clever money-getting rogue, but in his heart he knows that it is all a childish game; he has not lost his soul.

Let me add a comment on the newly appointed Simon Commission.

The outcry against the said Commission may seem very strange and foolish. It may be dismissed as the work of agitators and as wounded pride. No!—though I think that last explanation has some relation to the truth. To pretend that it is only the outcry of a few irresponsible agitators shows a complete misconception of the situation. To people in England I suppose the question of the Statutory Commission seems to be a matter of political expediency. To Indians it is no such thing. It is a crowning example of the almost invariable attitude of the British: an attitude of "damned superiority". "We know what is good for you." But every decent Indian is ready to reply: "We don't want your superior knowledge; it is our country, not yours; and we intend to manage it our own way." After all, it is one thing to act the benevolent uncle to a growing youth (say, the people of East Africa); but when it is a case of a rather seedy, middle-aged uncle who has seen a bit too much of life, patronizing an elderly relative who is just getting on to his feet again after a long illness, the resentment of the elder is hardly surprising.

When I left England I believed that India might become a contented, self-governing member of the British Commonwealth. I realized that it was quite a different proposition from that of French Canada, or Dutch South Africa, or even Ireland. All those peoples belong to the West and we recognize them—up to a point—as kindred people. But now I see how deep is the gulf that separates us from this great continent with its own civilization, of whose greatness the people are becoming increasingly conscious; and the real heart unity that a man like Andrews has established is very rare—with all respect to a number of the good missionaries.

It is not easy to form true judgments about a country like India, of such vast size, variety, and complexity. If I had spent all the last three months in the Friends' district in the Central Provinces living with the missionaries there, and facing their heart-breaking problems among the poor, immoral, untaught people, I should probably have very different things to say. It may well be that I have gone too far the other way. But, all the same, I believe that by living largely among Indians I have learned far more about their character in three months than many Englishmen seem to learn in thirty years. And I now say, as I should not have said three months ago, that our immediate duty to India is to hand over complete responsibility for the government of the country without delay. They must make their own Constitution, dealing with communalism and the Indian States and other things—such as the Assam tea-planters and Calcutta merchants—as best they can. That is our first duty. The second is infinitely more difficult and more painful: to learn to treat them as equals, and to respect them even when we find them misguided—perhaps even to show humble affection towards them, as they are only too ready to show to any white men who are willing to respond. It will be said that I take the wrath of the educated men of India as the voice of the people. Well, if I judge the nation by its cultured leaders, does not one do that of every nation? I wonder what the slaves and agriculturists and traders of Ancient Greece thought of the cultured few.

V

Also Written In Madras,
January 1928

Now for Assam and the goal of my ambition. Why it should have been so I cannot quite tell; but it was. And now that I have penetrated to the head of the Assam valley and returned again in safety, I feel as if the best part of my "mission" was fulfilled.

I think we will begin with a little amateur geography—physical and political. I hope it will have some relation to truth.

Everyone knows that the great Himalayan range of mountains forms the northern boundary of India. It is not so generally known that those mountains are, comparatively speaking, a mushroom growth, being almost wholly composed of limestone. How such inconceivable quantities of small animals can ever have lived upon the earth, and how, after their multitudinous lives and deaths, spreading over millions of years, they can have been forced up into that huge mountain mass, I leave the scientists to explain. Faith in science is great; otherwise such things must seem incredible.

The hills of Southern India are far more ancient; and ages after Southern India had come out of the sea a great upheaval took place, and two great arms rose up to the east and the west, raising on their shoulders, as it were, to the north the great Himalayan range. Here in Assam that range joins on to the eastern arm: or, if you like, the two are separated by the recently explored gorges of the Brahmaputra river. That river, having already traversed the highlands of Tibet for a thousand miles, descends by a series of mighty cascades and rapids to the low, flat valley of Assam, which lies between the Himalayas and the Naga and Khasia Hills. The valley is less than 500 feet above sea-level, throughout its length of nearly 500 miles; and it is nowhere 100 miles across. On the map, even a moderately large-scale map, it seems to be enclosed between the mountains. In reality, from most places the hills are remote or even invisible. At one point only, near Gauhati, some 350 miles down the valley, outliers of the mountain mass to the south occur beside (and even in) the river, and there are even some fine wooded hills on the north bank of the river.

There is no bridge across the Brahmaputra in its two-thousand-mile course—at any rate, there is none in the Indian thousand miles. In Upper Assam it shifts it course so much from year to year that even the shipping wharves are temporary structures and often have to be rebuilt after the rains. This year there were floods that did a good deal of damage to crops in one part. People spoke of 4-anna crops (25 per cent.), as in the drought of the Bolpur district in Bengal. The steamer connecting the railways crosses the river in the beautiful "narrows" just below Gauhati; but there the bottom is too deep for a bridge.

Assam was never conquered by the Moguls. Until the British conquest of Burma, whose king had recently conquered Assam, the Assamese had been for a long time outside India. Nevertheless, their religion is largely Hindu. I saw no traces of Buddhism in the Assam valley. The people mostly look more Indian than Mongolian, but many have strongly Mongolian features with Hindu colour. The hill tribes, south as well as north, are thoroughly Mongolian in appearance; they come down into the valley for marketing sometimes, also for "forced labour" on the roads—this raises some difficulties—and for labour on tea-gardens or in mines.

There are also immigrants who come from other parts of India for these purposes. Many have settled in their own little villages. Other localities include villages of hereditary fishermen. When the river is in flood many pools and water-courses get a fresh supply of fish; then the water recedes, leaving the fish in the pools; and one of the common sights of Assam is to see whole families or villages, men, women, boys, girls, small children, splashing and wading about in muddy pools or streams—sometimes in what is nothing but mud—"fishing" with inferior-looking nets, or even with their hands. They are said to spend hours waist-deep in the water; and in December, when a cold fog lies over many parts of the valley till 10 or 11 in the morning, it looks a chilly business.

The country is very productive. In Lower Assam I believe four crops can be got from the land in the year: one of flax, two of rice, and a mustard crop in the dry season (late winter). The rainfall is heavy; just to the south of the Khasia Hills is Cherrapunji, the wettest spot on earth (so far as is known), with a rainfall of nearly 500 inches in the year. I did not go there! Even in the dry season, as I have said, there is a nightly fog; this dampness makes possible the cultivation of tea.

Why, it may be asked, if the country is so productive, do not the Assamese people increase and multiply and flourish exceedingly? Are they inherently lazy? That is the reason hasty white men are fond of giving in such circumstances. I cannot say that I noticed any inherent laziness in those who took me about and cared for me. I believe an important part of the answer is contained in the one word "opium". Take India as a whole, and the opium problem is a minor concern, chiefly to be dealt with as a side issue of child welfare and other social improvements. Take the Assam valley alone and it is one of the gravest problems of the country. Everyone that I talked to agreed to this: the Governor himself and the Excise Minister (a Christian missionary belonging to the Khasia hill-tribes, lately turned politician), Swarajist leaders, respectable old Rai Bahadurs, minor officials and tea-planters, British and Assamese, down to the opium-consumers themselves and even perhaps the opium-sellers. They do not all agree as to the remedy. That is another matter, on which I have formed views of my own.

Opium is not the only thing they suffer from, though it may be the oldest, for the Assamese race have been under its influence for about a century. With the development of tea-gardens and the introduction of "foreign" labour various diseases began to rampage through the country; malaria became worse than it had ever been before, and the dread *kala-azar,* or black fever (not black-water fever)—one of the most fatal diseases in the world, I believe—appeared and swept through the country. It is now being combated with some success, and a League of Nations party of health experts, including my father's friend, the great Dr. Wu Lien Teh, whom I met attending the Eastern Congress of Tropical Medicine in Calcutta, is just going there to find out all about it.

Such are some of the sorrows of the Assamese. In 1921, at the time of the Non-co-operation movement, Gandhi visited Assam, and appealed to the people to abstain from opium and drink. Numbers of the better-class people, by a great effort of will, broke themselves from the habit—I met one or two of these people. Consumption dropped by nearly one-half in the year. The Government claim some part in this decrease, as they instituted some limiting measure about the same time, following the (then unpublished) "Botham" report of, I think, 1912; but I do not think there is the least doubt that the real job was done by Gandhi and the other workers whom he inspired. Of course, one of the main objects was to rob the Government of its excise; consequently these temperance workers were nearly all imprisoned. Most of them are still the recognized leaders of the Assam people—fine men, who have been purified by their suffering. But, I am sorry to say, they are reluctant to repeat their experiment till they have some guarantee of better treatment. Even if they simply preached temperance they are sure the police would make false charges against them. As so often in India, one is up against the abominations of the corrupt police system.

But they have not been sitting still. In 1924 C. F. Andrews got the Indian National Congress to appoint a special committee of inquiry—it was to have been the first of a series, but it has remained unique—to investigate the whole position. They were all Assamese, chiefly my hosts of last month, except for C. F. Andrews himself, who joined them after their preliminary investigation. They did their work with amazing thoroughness, and presented an unanswerable report, which the Government has never tried to challenge.

The secretary of that Committee was Rohinikanta Hatibarua (his surname indicates that his ancestors were the chief elephant-keepers to the old kings of Assam). He is a young member of the Provincial Council; and it was he who kindly took me round Assam last month.

Back to narrative. We left Calcatta on the afternoon of December 7th. Next morning, at daylight, we were getting into Lower Assam. I looked out to the north—we were running east—and, behold! a distant wall of mountains, the great Himalayas themselves. As the light increased I saw an occasional snowy peak through a gap in the nearer ranges; but in the main they were not snowy, and they were really rather disappointing. Of course, they were far away; and, anyway, they really were the mountains! In the afternoon, having crossed the river, we reached Gauhati. Here we only stayed for a few hours, calling on a particularly attractive, open-hearted man, who gave me his blessing for coming so far to co-operate in saving his people from this curse of opium.

Then we took the afternoon train through the night to Jorhat—a slow journey all round the Mikir and Rengma Hills. The chief excitement of this journey was the total eclipse of the moon. The moon was almost at the zenith—the eclipse being from 9.30 to 12 by Indian time—and I could see it by leaning out of the train at either side. Totality lasted for about half an hour. When the moon was nearly covered it turned a wonderful copper colour, and one edge remained so yellow that it hardly looked like a total eclipse. But all the stars round about it shone brilliantly; and as soon as the shadow began to pass the brilliant light of the uncovered edge was quite different from the dull yellow of totality. The earth's shadow as it moved across the moon looked practically straight.

As we passed through villages the people were marching up and down making a fine noise, "to frighten the dragon away". This sort of religious festival certainly provides the youth of the country with a glorious opportunity to make an infernal din. Any dragon with half an ear for music would slink into the jungle and die at the sound. The jungle! Yes, for the first time I really began to see what I had expected to see all over India: real jungle, with impenetrable undergrowth, huge bamboos, tall trees rising high above the seething swirl of vegetation, and enormous creepers striving to clamber to the tops of the trees, or hanging in festoons from the lower branches. Such places might—and no doubt did—contain many hidden tigers and other beasts. Even elephants might pass unseen a few yards away. Indeed, once from the train I heard a shout, and saw two little Tumais on the necks of two enormous elephants in the jungle quite near; but for the shout I should not have noticed them.

Early in the morning of the 9th the train stopped once. I was sleepy after the eclipse. But I later heard some English schoolgirls who were on the train saying that there had been a rogue elephant on the line in the fog. I do not know who drove it off. Rather later that morning Hatibarua observed at one station, "Now we go through the jungle for seven miles before we see anything else"; and it was so—not that I could have guessed the exact number of miles. Few jungle flowers were out; but there was, none the less, a wealth of colour, and an almost bewildering sense of intricate life, almost stifling, in all this jungly country.

Then, too, we began to see tea-gardens. The tea-plant grows wild in the jungles as a tall, scraggy bush with rather beautiful white flowers. Cultivated, it is kept down to two or three feet high, and is pruned right back when the leaf-picking season is over—in December. Only the fresh leaves are picked. So an extensive tea-garden shows you a great expanse of neat round bushes, usually with a few tall forest trees left to give some shade. The tea-gardens are nearly all on cleared jungle, some distance from the river. Nearer the river are vast stretches of paddy or rice-fields—in December a beautiful russet colour, just ready to be cut.

The railway up the Assam valley serves the tea-gardens rather than the towns. The towns lie on little old lines that run down to the river, for until quite recently the river was the chief means of communication. The new Government line is a good way south of the river in most places, and the small old lines built by the tea companies in their early days now run from main line to river, through the chief towns.

After parts of two days at Jorhat, where we paid a number of calls and visited two opium shops, we were motored twenty miles to Sibsagar, thus avoiding a tedious journey up to the main line and back again. It was an interesting drive. We passed some very large and beautiful tanks, built by the kings of Assam about 400 years ago, when they lived in a palace at Sibsagar (the palace we also saw); and for a mile or two before reaching Sibsagar we passed great stretches of watery country where every Englishman goes shooting at Christmas-time. There were pelicans, adjutant storks, white herons, ducks, and all kinds of things. Unluckily we could not stop.

But the road! It is the main road of Assam. In the rains it must be practically impassable. Now, in the dry weather, it was unspeakably bumpy. In places it was being "mended"; that is to say, large solid sods were cut from beside the ditches and heaped on the top of the road. Our car (a Ford or Overland—I forget now which), though accustomed to such things, had to stop and begin again at one or two of these places. An Englishman at Jorhat, a graduate of Birmingham, who, with his wife, also a Birmingham science graduate, looks after the scientific research station of the Tea-Gardens Association, showed me a report he had prepared for improving the roads of Assam. I hope the Government and the Swarajists will both accept his proposals. He also showed me photographs of people walking along the main road in the rainy season. It looked like one of the fishing parties already mentioned.

We had great luck at Sibsagar. In the afternoon on the day after our arrival we were just going to pay some calls when we met an ancient legal luminary, to whom I had to be introduced. He thereupon invited us to attend a tea party to which he was just going. It was a farewell party to an education official named Bardolai, brother of the man we had met at Gauhati. He was just moving to another town. Our venerable friend, being the doyen of the local bar, felt abundantly justified in inviting us. So we went, and met all the local celebrities; and, of course, they turned me into a sort of guest of honour, with their usual charming politeness. The real guest of honour, Mr. Bardolai, was a graduate of Birmingham. We talked at cross purposes for some little time, as he assumed I was a lecturer at Birmingham University, though I had told him I was not. (By the way, I have often noticed that if an Indian starts off with an erroneous idea in his head it takes some patience and tact to eradicate it. I think the language difficulty is partly responsible. Even those who are accustomed to use English in daily intercourse very rarely appreciate our fine shades. I am sure we tend greatly to underestimate the difficulty under which they constantly labour by having to try and use an alien language with alien thought-forms.) At last he realized his mistake, and it penetrated his mind, reaching a buried memory that there was a missionary college he had visited. "What was it called?" "Kingsmead," I suggested. "Yes, Kingsmead, of course—that is right; and the principal of the college—he was a fine man, a great big man, and very kind. He used to invite us to come and meet his students, so that they might learn something direct from the East before they came here. Yes, he was a fine man. What was his name?"

His memories of Mr. Hoyland and Kingsmead quite excited him. It seemed as though he remembered that England was not such a bad place after all, since it had contained such a man.

Later I was talking to the prison doctor about the effects of prison without opium on opium addicts, when I suddenly found that speeches were beginning. A dry little old man was addressing the guest of honour—in Assamese, of course. But I had hardly realized he was speaking when he finished his speech. The response was equally brief. But then at its end Mr. Bardolai broke into English, and told his friends how I had reminded him of Mr. Hoyland and Kingsmead, and so I had awakened a host of happy memories. This led to a request that I should say something. But having had such excellent examples of the "inevitable long-windedness of all Indian speeches", I took the hint, and only said how glad I had been to find that Mr. Bardolai had such happy memories of Kingsmead, and that it had been a great privilege and honour to be present. Three speeches within two minutes (or even one) must surely be a record, not only for India!

My host at Sibsagar lived in a house at the end of an oval lane that led nowhere beyond, so that he was practically in the jungle. He told me that one night his brother smelt a tiger, and had a shot at it in the dark; I presume there was something more than the smell to aim at. One night while I was there the jackals came very near and made an extraordinary noise. I wondered if this meant that they were mobbing a tiger; but I smelt no smell. Early each morning, before Hatibarua came for me, I had delightful walks along the grassy track in the fog. Many birds are found in Assam that do not occur in the plains of India. I had noticed in *The Fauna of British India,* which I consulted in Calcutta, that there were numbers of Indian sun-birds with all sorts of gorgeous colours; but I had only seen two—both common in the plains. No sooner did I reach Assam than I began to see the others. Indeed, I saw one "jewelled mite" (I am sure that is the right expression) on a wire by a railway station behind the Rengma Hills. It had a gorgeous red breast—almost carmine. At Sibsagar I found several more of these exquisite creatures. The morning after the tea party I had wandered rather farther than before into the region of houses, and was gazing up into the tree-tops when I found that a small crowd had gathered. My behaviour seemed to them unusual for the English kind, and apparently rather dubious; so they went to call a medical officer (I think) who could speak English. He recognized me from the tea party, and tried to make suitable conversation about birds; but, like most Indians, he was vague about any but the most ordinary species.

The Indian attitude towards birds is excellent. They leave them alone; and the birds respond by being more confiding than in any European country. But Indians seem to have no inquisitiveness about birds: they do not trouble to distinguish one from another, or study their habits. An Englishman who insists on finding out these things seems almost as strange to them—indeed, much stranger to-day—than one who slaughters all he sees. But, though it may be a queer Western kink, it is at least, I think they feel, a pardonable kink.

At Sibsagar I noticed football posts and some Indian schoolboys kicking a ball about. So, said I, the British religion has penetrated thus far. Surely the spread of football and hockey and tennis to the ends of the earth is the greatest testimony to the influence of the English spirit in the world to-day. It is curious that our national game, cricket, hardly spreads beyond the English countries. Even Americans seem to find no merit in it. So it is the more remarkable that young India—especially in the towns—seems to play cricket with as much zest as young England. Indeed, I had the fantastic idea, when I saw the Bombay *maidan* covered with cricketers after the day's work was done, that there must be more in common between British and Indians than is usually supposed. I suggest that the practical British have deep down in their nature a strain of quiet contemplation which a few of them have developed into Quakerism, while the majority prefer to sit in silence round a cricket ground, or to stand bareheaded in the field waiting for the ball that never comes, or the turn to bat which passes so quickly. We are shy about our innate mysticism, so we work it out in cricket; the Indians are less shy, so they have not needed to evolve cricket for themselves; but their mystical nature finds it attractive now that we have introduced it to them.

Next we went a stage farther up the valley, to Tinsukia, where the main line ends. Here we spent a night, and in the early morning visited another opium-stricken village; we had been to one near Sibsagar. We found the men, each in his miserable hovel (you can tell an opium addict's house at a glance from the others), smoking his morning pipe over a little fire of sticks, while his half-naked children stood shivering round, or tried to begin to do some of the work the incapable father could no longer do. And it was here at Tinsukia, too, that we saw the most pathetic opium victim: a youth of twenty-one, a beggar, unable to walk on his legs, who took such a heavy daily dose that he required half as much again as the maximum monthly allowance under the new rationing system. This he gets from the opium-vender out of what remains over from short-weight sold to other customers. He spends nearly a rupee a day on opium; but easily gets that much by begging. This opium shop was close to the railway station and junction. If you reflect upon this tale it reveals many things.

Also I must tell another pathetic tale—a different kind of pathos—about a local excise officer. We went to call on him without warning, and when I began to ask him questions he was very hesitating in his answers. At first I suspected language difficulty; but it was soon obvious that he was appalled at this sudden visitation of a Swarajist politician and a quite unknown Englishman. After a little more hesitation he said appealingly: "Do you mind if I come and see you alone at the Dak bungalow in an hour or two? I can answer your questions then." Now, it is notorious that these excise officers are very corrupt. There is a lot of drug smuggling; and many of them undoubtedly share in the profits from the smuggling trade. Two hours later (according to appointment) he duly came; he had thought out the proper answers and gave them. Then he said: "Will you please tell me what you think we ought to do to get rid of the opium?" "No," said I, "I can't tell you that. I haven't come here to tell you what to do, but only to encourage you and everyone who is trying to get rid of it." And after a little more talk, at parting he said rather pathetically: "I really am trying to do my best for my country." It was a good deal for him to use that phrase; and I took it that he was answering the accusations, not that I had brought against him, but in his own conscience. His very transparent double-mindedness and his attempt to struggle against it seemed to me tragic—and perhaps heroic, too.

I saw an Indian's tea-garden at Tinsukia, and a very large European one under an enlightened English manager; and we stayed for a few days with an Indian tea-planter near Dibrugarh: this man was an Edinburgh M. A., recently returned from the West, whose Western veneer had not quite worn off. Poor fellow, he had single-handed to entertain Messrs. Purcell and Hallsworth as well as myself. They arrived the day after me, to see the conditions of the tea-garden coolies and the miners, of whom more shortly.

We were invited to a Hindu wedding. There I talked to a Hindu missionary from Kashmir—a fine man, with a very pure religious idealism; he had ruined his health in disease-stricken

Assam, but he had started three homes with a religious basis for orphans. He was a great respecter of the best side of the West, and I should say very friendly to true Christianity. He introduced me to an "atheist" friend, one who thought it so important for men to live well here on earth that they had better give up speculating and quarrelling about God, whom they had not seen, until they had learnt to love the brother whom they had seen—a kind of "atheism" for which I have plenty of sympathy. Neither of these men had any use for the formalism and vulgar mummery of this marriage service.

Next day we visited the coal-mines of Margherita, and then I started down the valley again. But no, it was not next day, and I must not omit the last evening at Dibrugarh, when I refused, on grounds of health, to speak at a public meeting for which I had been advertised—Purcell and Hallsworth were quite enough—and had a peaceful walk at sunset by the great river Brahmaputra. I watched pied kingfishers plunging in the water and little waders running on the mud; and heard great splashes of probable crocodiles; then the sun went down behind the Himalayas and a red glow was reflected in the broad water; and the earth was filled with peace—or was it only my heart?

Now, then, we set off again for Margherita, via Tinsukia. But our host gave us such a fine early breakfast that the train started just as we reached the station; and it had to be called back again—all this in the fog and gloom just before dawn. On the way to Margherita a place called Digboi is passed, where are the hideous erections man places over those parts of the earth from which oil is tapped. So I have seen a real live oil-well, the only one at present working successfully in Assam. I believe 20,000 men are employed at it. Margherita is on the edge of the unknown. You come to the foot of the hill, and the mine-shaft runs straight beyond you into the hill-side: it goes straight along not down; and above you rise the hills covered with impenetrable jungle, in which live all manner of wild beasts and wild men, all across to Burma. Rumour says these hills are full of minerals; other rumour says that the right of exploitation is already assigned to European firms, over thousands of square miles of unadministered country. I wonder!

Our host, the manager of the mine, formerly an Indian Civil Service man in the Punjab, but "retired" after Amritsar, seemed to me an amiable man; he had a pleasant way with the two Indians in our party, and rallied Hatibarua gaily over some of their political strifes.

One of the coal-mines is a quarry with a 40-foot seam visible, and 90 feet more below the surface. I thought it looked poor coal, and so apparently did Mr. Purcell. Hatibarua, of course, disliked all this foreign exploitation of his country, and argued the point with our host, who said it was bringing lots of wealth into the country. "And all the problems of industrial and city life", was, in effect, Hatibarua's reply.

It was strange to see the devices and engines of civilization here jostling with the primeval jungle. My sentiments are all with the jungle!

In the Assam valley I only talked to one British official. He made me very angry. If he thought he was combating the impression that my Swarajist friends would have made upon me, he was sadly misguided; what he said had exactly the opposite effect. It is annoying to be treated as a perfect fool when you have not even been given the chance of showing whether you are one or not. However, I must allow him all the excuses I can. In the first place, Purcell and Hallsworth came with me, so he was 1 to 3. Then, he asked us to come at 3 o'clock—local time is fifty-four minutes in advance of Indian standard time—and we went by the latter, and I think he had been waiting nearly an hour. Also a very misleading paragraph about me had appeared in the *Times of Assam;* and although he incidentally told us what an unreliable paper it was, he had probably read it and believed it. He spent much of his time reviling the Assamese people, and especially the politicians; and an unfortunate Indian official, his junior, had to sit and hear it all, and occasionally say "Yes" when appealed to to confirm some foolish allegation. He was never given the opportunity to say "No". Perhaps the most fantastic statement was that the Chinese Government (he did not say which) was now trying to flood India with opium, having first cunningly persuaded the Government of India to give up the export of opium to China. In fact, nearly all the opium that is smuggled into Assam is Malwa opium, and both at Calcutta and Madras I was told by responsible officials that Malwa opium forms almost, if not quite, 100 per cent. of the smuggled drug. He also made silly statements about the opium-smoking habit in Assam; and he had never heard of the Viceroy's meeting with the Malwa princes last June. His most revealing statement was that wherever he went news of his coming spread, so he could never see things as they really were.

If this man had alone represented British officialdom in Assam to me, I should certainly have carried away a very bad impression. But I had an introduction to the Governor, Sir Laurie Hammond, and before leaving Assam I made an expedition to Shillong to see him. Assam Province includes some poor districts of Eastern Bengal, south of the Khasia Hills, and so the capital has been placed near the top of the hills, at a height of 5,000 feet. It is a glorious place (at any rate, when the sun is shining), with magnificent views of snowy Himalayan peaks, perhaps 200 miles to the north. A splendid road has been built from Gauhati, and there is a daily service of motor-buses. I think the road would occupy quite a respectable place in any list of the world's beautiful roads. There is great variety of scenery: first some miles of dense jungle, in places on steep slopes, with little, rushing torrents falling down the hill-sides; then, after many twists and turns, there comes a comparatively level, grassy region with barren, rocky hill-tops; and, after that, more steep, wooded slopes with pine-trees in ever-increasing numbers. In spite of the badly sprung motor-bus I enjoyed the whole of the sixty-mile, four-hour drive.

At Shillong I had a glorious morning's walk in the woods. It happened to be market day; and as I started out I met hundreds of little hill-people, in a continual stream, coming down from the higher parts of the hills to their eight-day market—men and women alike with huge loads in long baskets on their backs, held in place by a strap across the forehead. Most of these would consist of potatoes, but I heard fowls clucking in a few of the baskets. These little people came trotting down the slopes with a curious, gentle, tripping motion, their knees bent all the time. The eight-day interval is curious, and suggests an eight-day week among the hill tribes. I do not know if it is found outside the Khasia Hills. Apparently the Christians, of whom there are many, do not come when the market is on Sunday; so when a Monday market comes I suppose they must bring sixteen days' produce with them. It seems rather unfair! Some have to come twenty or thirty miles. I suppose they carry equally heavy loads back with them. There is a Pasteur Institute in Shillong, and every market day scores of people come to get inoculated against rabies, which is very prevalent in the hills.

As the stream of people seemed to be endless I turned off by side-tracks. Suddenly through the trees I saw the far-off chain of snowy peaks high in the sky, sharp and clear above the dusty cloud that always hangs in the valley. I believe somebody has proved that but for refraction you could not see the Himalayas at all from Shillong. So much the better for refraction.

Soon I found myself in deep, silent jungle; but it was not all silent. Here and there I came upon great roving parties of little birds. I always associate the crowds of little tits and goldcrests that one can often find in English woods with soft December days; and in spite of the different climate these little birds seemed very home-like. There were tits here, some almost like our common great-tit; little tiny willow-warblers with barred wings to replace our goldcrest at home; an occasional woodpecker, not unlike one of our "spotteds". But here, too, were gorgeous little flower-peckers; brilliant red minivets; black and yellow bulbuls; little brown babblers, half hedge-sparrow and half crested tit; and, most curious, in one place a flock of blackbirds, yellow-billed like ours, but silent, furtive creatures. I wanted weeks and months to spend among these birds, and I had only these few hours, snatched between visits to high officials. It was fascinating; it was tantalizing.

Talks with officials at Shillong I may not record. The upshot seems to be that Government and popular leaders cannot work together to-day; there is too much mutual suspicion. So social reform is scarcely possible—or, at least, seriously hampered.

I shall never forget my fortnight in Assam. India is immense and unfathomable; Assam, by contrast, compact and straightforward.

VI

MADRAS,
January 1928

From Assam I travelled to Darjeeling, and met my father-in-law at 2.30 a.m. at a junction. As we were due at 6 a.m. on the 22nd at the foot of the mountains, where the ordinary railway ends, we were up betimes; and while we were dressing I suddenly noticed the great snowy range of Kinchinjunga ahead of us, all rosy with the first glow of the rising sun. It was a great sight, finer, said my father-in-law, than the dawn on Monte Rosa from the plains of Lombardy.

We motored instead of going up by the mountain railway: a 50-mile drive and a rise of over 7,000 feet. It was fine country, but the road is less beautiful than the Gauhati–Shillong road, and a good deal more populous, especially near the top, so I was rather spoilt for it. At Ghoom, two and a half miles from Darjeeling, the ridge is reached, and then there is a slight downhill to Darjeeling, which is on a northern spur, looking straight across to the mighty Kinchinjunga. The top of the mountain is over 40 miles from Darjeeling, and in the clear atmosphere it does not look its full height. If I had been told it was 15,000 feet high (instead of 28,000 feet) I should have believed it; and I had imagined it much more of a peak than it is. The snowline on the southern side is high even in winter, and the glaciers are mostly hidden by shoulders of the mountain. From Darjeeling you look down vast slopes into remote valleys, then across to other dark mountain slopes, and finally up to the snowy heights. After midday a cloudy belt tended to form near the snow-line, and this seemed to lift the mountain up into the sky, making it far more lofty. At dawn, and at sunset too, when the light was not too strong, the rosy glow gave the mountain an aspect of remoteness and immensity. At sunset, especially, the sunlight seemed to linger an incredible time on the higher slopes, till the valleys far below were lost in the darkness of night.

We had brilliant weather, and the sun was hot at noon, but not with the dangerous heat of the Tropics. I found it quite safe to go hatless, though I was rather careful not to let the midday sun shine for long on the back of my neck. At night there was frost, and I noticed one very sheltered north-facing path, under 7,500 feet, where there was frost still at 3 o'clock in the afternoon.

The proper thing is to go up Tiger Hill (three miles from Ghoom) and see the sunrise glow on Mount Everest, over a hundred miles away. At Christmas-time this would have been a cold opportunity, and we preferred to catch a 9.30 train to Ghoom and walk up through the woods during the morning. It is a beautiful walk, and after we left Ghoom we hardly saw a human being. The day was perfect; no cloud formed on the nearer mountain ranges to conceal the summit of Everest. It was my father-in-law who first noticed the snowy summit through the trees. From the top of Tiger Hill you see the summit and a shoulder of the mountain to the north of it, the great eastern precipices face you, and two lesser peaks to the south are also visible.

On Christmas Day there was a great fair at Darjeeling. The market-place was filled with people from all over the country: Nepalese, Tibetans, and other hill people, mostly Mongolian in feature (as all the hill people are) and wearing all kinds of marvellous costumes: some with pigtails, some wearing square hats with furry corners, some in moccasin-like shoes, and the women in many gaudy colours, magenta being one of the most popular.

At Darjeeling we were in a Buddhist country. We saw several Buddhist temples, and their prayer flags were hanging in festoons in all sorts of sacred places, and especially at the shrine on Observatory Hill. This has a wonderful view across to Kinchinjunga, and its choice as a special Buddhist shrine suggests to me that the people are not quite as indifferent to the magic awe of their country's scenery as is commonly supposed. The prayers fly in the breeze and so are wafted heavenwards. When they are finally washed clean, or blanched by rain and wind and sun, I believe the sins of the man who offered the prayer are expiated. They are said to be often in indelible ink. Is this encouraged by the priests, or is it due to a desire not to reach Nirvana (if that is the goal) too soon?

On Christmas Day we saw several poor peasants giving their offerings to the fat priests, and performing the ritual of walking round and round the shrine: apparently sheer ignorant superstition, exploited by priests with an eye to good business. The priests certainly looked and behaved as if they had no thought of anything spiritual or elevating. A man sitting on the ground near by, reading his Scriptures, seemed to have a much gentler, more refined countenance. Once again I was impressed by the sight of so-called religion as the worst enemy of true religion.

In order to see anything at all of the Indian National Congress I had to leave Darjeeling at midday on Christmas Day. Thus I reached Madras early on the 28th, in time only for the last day of the Congress. Real discussion only took place in the Subjects Committee held just before the Congress, and this I missed altogether. Nevertheless, I saw and heard much of great interest. Two incidents of my journey southwards may be worth mentioning, as I fear they are symptomatic. Some little way down from Darjeeling an English girl (say, twenty), who was alone in the compartment next to mine, confided that an Indian from the next compartment had spoken to her. She had never travelled alone in India before, and was obviously terrified of the "horrid, dreadful man". From what I saw of him I am sure he was merely incurably anxious to be friendly. Then an Englishman with whom I travelled from Calcutta to Madras told me in the morning that one of the Indians in the compartment had got up in the night and begun to put his hands into the Englishman's clothes. Now, as it happens I was awake, too, and though I could not understand why the Indian stood for some time in the middle of the compartment, I am quite sure he did no such thing. It was simply the Englishman's incurable suspicion of all Indians that led him to imagine it.

This lack of discrimination and of insight has appalling consequences.

After breakfast on the 28th F. H. G. took me to the Congress. We first attended a meeting of the Social Conference (dozens of subsidiary conferences take place while the Congress is on), and we came in for two very interesting speeches. Shaukat Ali, one of the two famous Muslim brothers, a great big bearded man, was supposed to be speaking in support of a motion against the rigid enforcement of *purdah*. Actually he spoke all the time, warning the women present (there were large numbers) of the dangers of losing their modesty, and extolling *purdah* as the best system for upholding a proper feminine modesty and purity. He was followed by Mrs. Sarojini Naidu, the most popular and effective of Indian woman orators. She had been sitting on the platform behind Shaukat Ali; and she explained that she had not heard a word he said, but she knew quite well what he always said; and she proceeded to explain what he really meant. According to Mrs. Naidu, Shaukat Ali, in extolling *purdah,* had been thinking, not of the system of inhibitions which are the outward expressions of the conventional idea of *purdah,* but of that essential modesty and grace and purity of mind which are the attributes of all true womanliness. And she proceeded to argue forcibly that with the destruction of the present *purdah* regulations the relations of men and women might achieve a purity based on knowledge and conviction, instead of an unreal purity based on artificial restrictions and conventions. I could not hear everything she said. I believe it was she who suggested that if *purdah* were such an excellent institution as some men seemed to think the men might adopt it for themselves and leave the women free.

By this time the Congress proper had begun its session and we moved to the Congress tent. This was a vast erection, a sort of thatched tent supported on great poles, estimated to hold 15,000 people. I dare say it would hold more. Mr. Sen Gupta told me that 50,000 were present at the Congress ground the first day. I do not know how he could tell. Certainly many thousands were in attendance; how many from other parts of India I cannot say. A man from Madura, with whom I travelled a week later, said it was the largest Congress he had ever attended. Mr. Sen Gupta said they had once had a bigger one. The Madura man said it was far more representative of many classes (in our Western sense), as well as creeds and castes, than any recent Congress. All this is due, of course, to the practically universal desire of all educated and moderately intelligent Indians to unite in the most energetic protest against the purely British Statutory Commission. Several English people have assured me that, whereas feeling had been gradually improving since 1921, now the alienation and resentment are only comparable to the non-co-operation days. It is widely believed that the Viceroy advised a different procedure. I regard this as testimony to the universal respect for his character.

Discussion of the Statutory Commission was over. Resolutions for a complete boycott of it, and directing the Committee to work for full independence, had been unanimously passed.

A number of resolutions were still to be brought forward. The most important of these, on Hindu-Muslim relations, was now under discussion. We bought ordinary visitors' tickets, and entered the tent at the far end from the platform. There were a number of loud-speakers, or amplifiers, or whatever they are called. But the one nearest to us was too far off, so we could hear nothing. So we went round to the other side, behind the platform, and I sent in my card to Mr. Sen Gupta (he had kindly suggested my doing so), and he brought us in to sit among Congress leaders on the platform. We were behind the speakers, but close to an amplifier which, though rather tinny, was effective. Also I got a copy of the resolutions and could talk quietly to Mr. Sen Gupta and others. The resolution under discussion was very long, and carefully drawn: the first half proposed the abolition of communal constituencies for elections, with elaborate safeguards for minorities and a more natural division of provinces, which would be specially favourable to the Muslims in the case of Sind (which is still administered from Bombay). The second part admitted that, as Muslims claim the right to slaughter cows, and as Hindus claim the right to play music outside mosques (the two things that actually cause most communal outbreaks), they should not be prohibited from doing these things; but it was an appeal to each community to respect the other, and not to go to law or call in the British authorities.

The Congress is, of course, predominantly Hindu; but this year a Muslim was president and several of the Muslim leaders were participating. Several Hindu leaders objected to the second part of the resolution, pointing out that their objection to cow-slaughter is a religious objection, whereas Muslims have no religious objection to music. The first part of the resolution was not questioned. Mr. Sen Gupta then intervened. He had been one of the group that drafted the resolution, so he understood its exact significance. It was a remarkably able speech. I am sure if he is ever a responsible Minister he will be capable of persuading his followers to accept measures they really detest. He pointed out that in the past attempts had been made to reach a compromise, but it was never more than a paper agreement; this resolution was based on a different conception. It involved no surrender of position: what was mutually recognized was not the right to do certain things, but the claim to that right—a claim which no one could deny. The resolution was an appeal for mutual respect and mutual confidence. As such it was finally carried without opposition.

It is interesting to notice that at the Muslim League Conference, since held in Calcutta, the first part of the resolution alone aroused opposition; and it was only passed with the proviso that Sind must first be constituted as a separate province. The Muslim League seems to have been more suspicious in its attitude than the Congress. Of course, it represents the chief minority.

At the afternoon session several other resolutions were passed. I sat in a good place called "Complimentary". A resolution calling on the Congress Committee to invite other political bodies to form a joint committee to draft an Indian Constitution for submission to an All-India representative conference, to be held in March at Delhi, was opposed by a few members on the ground that independence should first be achieved. This is probably good psychology, if unity is to be kept; but the more honest attitude—that some definition of "independence" is required—carried the day. Another important and carefully worded resolution dealt with the position of the Indian States in an independent India; it appealed to the Indian princes to show their friendliness to the cause of independence by adopting democratic institutions; and also warned them of the danger of continuing their autocratic rule.

I thought it rather pathetic that no one ventured to combat the sophistries lying behind a resolution for the discriminatory boycott of British goods. Quite apart from economic arguments, I wished I could have appealed to the Congress to make it easier, not more difficult, to show the British public the reasonableness of India's claim. I was glad to see, subsequently, that Fenner Brockway, in his message to the Congress, had said something like this. But the Congress as a whole, and even its leaders, are in no mood now for such an argument. As one of the leaders said to me later: "First we believed in the British officials as a whole; then in the higher officials; then in the Viceroy; then in the British Government; then in Parliament; then in the Labour Party. All have failed. Now we only believe in our own efforts." They recognize a few I.L.P. idealists as their only remaining friends in England. But they judge them (or us) to be few, feeble, and helpless. Perhaps they are right.

The leader I have just quoted was Mr. Srinivasa Iyengar, the retiring President. Mr. Iyengar is an elderly man, and he was very tired after all his exertions. It had been, in effect, his Congress. But he was very happy. Some years ago he was the Advocate General in the Government of Madras, but he has been going farther and farther to the left; and he assured me that in spite of his weariness he felt very young and ready for any adventure. It was natural, of course, that he should be in a state of exaltation. I asked him what steps they would take to achieve independence. In effect, he expounded a "Sinn Fein" policy: establishment of their own assemblies, councils, courts, etc., and refusal to use the British institutions.

To all intents and purposes this is non-co-operation over again, without a Mahatma to lead the common people in its support; but, on the other hand, with a widely convinced *intelligentsia,* and they were Gandhi's chief stumbling-block. Srinivasa Iyengar explained that Gandhi's campaign made the idea of suffering too central: "We are ready to suffer again, but not for the sake of suffering. We shall try to achieve some concrete result, and if we are imprisoned for that we shan't mind." Whether the younger generation is really prepared for all this I cannot judge; I believe they think they are. Only the event can prove whether they have the courage and endurance and capacity for this high adventure.

The day after the Congress was "Women's Day", and the evening Congress was open to men. I went and found it was in the big tent; but no one on the outskirts of the tent was trying to listen, and at first I thought I should hear nothing. At last I pressed forward among a crowd of Indian men who were standing close under the rostrum, and here I could both see and hear the speakers quite well, except the chairwoman, a dignified lady who is vice-president of the Madras Provincial Council. She was unfortunately quite inaudible, so that the putting of resolutions was even more of a farce than in the Congress. Moreover, only the women could vote, and they were all behind her. A number of resolutions were moved, seconded, and carried, and the speeches were all excellent. None was wordy, like most of the men's speeches the day before. Each woman knew what she wanted to say, said it, and sat down. Most of the resolutions were in favour of equality for women: equal wages for equal work, equal inter-sex rights, equal political rights. One or two youths near me found the resolution on sex rather amusing, but with this exception the crowd was thoroughly attentive, respectful, and sympathetic. It was a really impressive occasion. The last resolution was in favour of international peace—on humanitarian and "motherly" grounds. The young men of India are in no mood to listen to Englishmen who plead for peace, so I wondered how they would take it. Most unfortunately the first speech was inaudible and the second was in Tamil; so I came away in the middle of the latter; the crowd was melting away. I might mention, though, that Mr. Iyengar, who asked me a lot of questions about England and Europe, and especially about the prospects of an Anglo-Russian war, dissociated himself strongly from those of his fellow countrymen who see hope for their country's liberty in such a conflict.

I saw a good deal of H. while I was in Madras. He was still in rooms at the Club, so I could not stay with him. I found him less detached than on shipboard, and utterly sceptical of the capacity of the Indians to turn any of their fine speeches into action. It is doubtless true (and an important truth) that a man who is working with Indians all the time learns many things about them that a passing visitor cannot learn; though I think the opposite is also true. In spite of my respect for H. I was not reconverted by him. I think he, like others though in less degree, has got into the way of thinking that outward appearance is more significant than in fact it is. I suspect that a spirit is working in India which they do not perceive. Whether it will come to its fruition soon or late may be a matter for dispute; I am inclined to think it will come soon and lead to rude awakenings. Would that it might come without violence or bloodshed!

Although I am not reconverted to what W. F. S. calls the "imperialism" of my first letters from India, I cannot put out of my mind the vision of 700,000 Indian villages almost untouched by the politicians and the *intelligentsia;* and still, I think, looking to the British (and more particularly to the missionaries where there are any) rather than to their own leaders for any escape from their misery. If we were really fulfilling the mission of Christian liberators to these millions of outcastes and half-starved peasants, the argument for remaining in India, in spite of all the opposition of the *intelligentsia,* would be enormously strong. But I am afraid we have largely failed. Or rather, perhaps, we have done all that we can do. We have sown the seed, but our Western methods of tending the crop will not do. If it is to ripen, those who know the nature of the soil must tend the crop, even though they seem to us incompetent.

As I have written before, the worst feature of the present system seems to me to be the almost complete lack of understanding or sympathy between the English and the educated Indian. So it was particularly delightful to stay with the G.s, who have evidently established sincere and simple friendship with many real Indians, who call on them freely and rejoice in their hospitality. I noticed that even Mr. Satyamurti, who at first offered to "show me Madras", and the editor of *The Hindu,* whom I also met, both seemed satisfied that as I was with Dr. G. I was in safe hands; and it is possible for him to achieve a position that for a missionary seems to me practically impossible. The large bungalow he lives in (which he dislikes) is the natural consequence of his position as superintendent of the museum. An Indian in the same position would have the same bungalow; whereas a missionary who is supposed to represent the Christ who "had not where to lay his head" cannot make the same appeal while he lives (as a married missionary must) in a European bungalow. The people among whom he lives *cannot* see the sacrifice he is making. They only see that he insists on living in a way that is impossible to them. Further, communal propaganda seems to them to be his main *raison d'etre* and makes him suspect of ulterior motives. People like the G.s are the real missionaries, only there is no place for them in rural India! What is the solution? I do not know. It ought to be the liberation of the depressed people of India by Indians who have a Christ-like spirit.

One afternoon F. H. G. and I went with an Indian Christian, a professor of science at one of the Madras colleges, to see some of the local temples. They are fine buildings. Our guide seemed to be a real Christian and a real Indian. Too many Indian Christians I have met seem to be neither. I think now that they are joining the ranks of their nationalist fellow countrymen they are tending to become better Christians, too.

D. H. took me over the Women's Christian College, so I had a chance to admire the new chapel. I think it is the most beautiful piece of architecture I have seen in India, dating from the British period. It belongs to its surroundings. It is a real masterpiece.

I was almost forgetting that I paid three visits to the Theosophical Headquarters at Adyar. First, a rather ineffectual attempt to make use of several introductions given me by T.: we had a few minutes' talk with the master of the school, but they were engrossed in an exciting hockey match—School *v.* Old Boys—which resulted in a draw, 1–1. Then we went the same evening to a wonderful musical recitation (alternate explanation and chanting) of an ancient Hindu story under the great Banyan-tree, one of the biggest in India. The story began with an absurdly trivial episode that involved the gods and men in all sorts of complications; we left before the end. It was an amateur performance by a professor of mathematics. He did it with great effect, and showed consummate skill in the finer shades of recitation.

Then finally, by appointment, I went to see the whole place under the guidance of one of the members, Mr. Prasad—a delightful man who never made me feel uncomfortable by obtruding theosophy. The whole place, and especially the school, impressed me in its emphasis on beauty. One of the good points about the school is that the children are housed as in their own villages; but they learn how to make the best of things, and how to beautify their surroundings by cultivating flowers, etc. There are girls as well as boys, and all castes live together. I understood that there were outcastes, but the G.s rather doubted this. If there are, it is certainly a great achievement for Southern India. I felt something of the Santiniketan spirit, but not all: Mrs. Besant is not Tagore. I think the school is the best part, the bookshop the worst; though I was glad to see copies of Miss Kelman's book in the Indian section.

I am still omitting all manner of interesting Madras events: A special library exhibition, opened by one of the most generally respected and capable Indian ministers, and a "private-view" with F. H. G. (whose office makes him head of one of the chief libraries) beforehand: all sorts of interesting ancient manuscripts, etc. Then also F. H. G. expounded to me some of the archaeological treasures of the museum. He is a real expert, but I am sure a Westerner must be trained to appreciate Indian sculpture. Also he showed me over the institute, where they sell beautiful things made in South India to-day; and one evening we saw part of a "dumb show" in the theatre at the museum. This, too, was an acted fable, the actors representing weird non-human creatures, wearing vast headgear and hoop-skirts. Most of these shows were special excitements of Congress week.

Before leaving Madras perhaps I ought to sum up my impressions of the Congress. It was, of course, too large for deliberation. The resolutions and speeches were chiefly interesting as showing the mentality of the leaders. But although the resolutions did not reflect the will of all the members in detail, it was impressive to realize that this vast concourse was due to a general sympathy, perhaps even a passionate sympathy, with the main purpose of the Congress, the achievement of a truly self-governing, responsible India, with a status at least equal to that of the great nations of the West. And I was impressed by the number—perhaps less than 10 per cent., but still considerable—of women, quiet, composed, self-confident, and taking a real part in the deliberations and decisions. I think it would have been good for Miss Mayo to have attended the Social Conference and the Women's Day.

After an interesting journey through South India—great temples at Tanjore and Madura, and others on strange rocky hills, two or three hours in the beautiful Palni Hills, a passing sight of the shrine of a goddess surrounded by mud-horses for her midnight rides, and other fine scenery—I crossed to Ceylon and reached Colombo, en route for Java and Malaya. My boat being a day late, I had two days to wait there, but I was weary of travel, so I did not visit Kandy; I have since heard that plague is very bad there. It is said to be a very beautiful journey, but I felt surfeited with beauties and wonders. A few days of monotonous sea will be a restful change.

I really learnt almost nothing about Ceylon, except that it is the gateway to Australia. My fellow passengers from Madras and the other inhabitants of the little hotel were nearly all Australians. The dishes were purposely described as Australian. An Australian schoolboys' cricket team was touring the country.

This I learnt from the one newspaper I bought. It also showed that the Ceylonese are learning the political language and methods of Nationalist India.

One afternoon I watched a lot of whiskered terns flitting over the lake; and in the beautiful Victoria Park I spent hours watching birds. There I saw my first male paradise flycatcher: an impossibly beautiful bird with black head and top-knot, otherwise pure white, with long white streamers extending from the tail. In the presence of such perfect loveliness political strife seems all *maya,* illusion. If I were ever to visit India again after this spring, I think it would be only to watch the minivets and bee-eaters and sun-birds, and perhaps to learn how to be silent.

VII

BETWEEN SUMATRA AND BANKA,
February 2, 1928

Twelve days have been, of course, hopelessly inadequate to learn what I wanted to learn about a country over 600 miles in length, inhabited by over 30,000,000 people. Still, I think the visit to Java has been worth while. Many Englishmen are in danger, I think (following Kipling), of thinking of "the East" in terms of British India alone, or of British possessions; and you meet too many English globe-trotters who are following an "all-red" route, and yet imagine that they are seeing the world. Of course, I ought to have seen Indo-China under the French, or independent Siam, which I am assured is a most progressive country—to say nothing of China and Japan and Korea and the Philippines and Borneo: but no, life is short and the world is large. My plan has been to study British India pretty closely (though even that is a foolish statement: what are five months for such a country?), and in the middle of that study to get away for a few weeks and get a fleeting picture of what the Dutch are doing in a rather similar (but also very different) position in Java, and now I am about to spend a similar time glancing at Malaya, which again is the East administered by the West, but a very different East. I might call my winter in the East one hasty sketch and two snapshots.

I think I ended my last journal on the boat from Colombo to Singapore. I need not add much about that voyage, but one or two things are worth mentioning. There was only one missionary on board, a Wesleyan from near Canton with his wife and small children. Like most people I meet in this world, he knew and respected H. G. Wood. He put me in touch with a

Hong-Kong police officer. This is the advantage one gets from second class travel. This man was no chief official who deals in statistics and Government measures, but one who knew the bad habits of the people at first hand. He had smoked in opium dens more than once. He was a little suspicious of me at first, but as I did not bombard him with questions he presently opened out in his own way. The two things he seemed anxious to impress upon me were: First, that a man could smoke opium for thirty years without his friends knowing it; secondly, that far more people in Hong-Kong are ruined by spirits than by opium. The evening we were in Penang he drove this home. They had been unloading gin and brandy in great packing-cases from our hold all day long; they were still doing it. He pointed this out to me. At first, taking the ordinary white man's pose, he said how sad it was to see all that stuff leaving the boat; why would not they let him have one to take home? It would keep him going for a year. But then he added: "No, I don't really want it; it's a *bad brand.*" (Perhaps it is just as well that I do not remember the name of the brand!) And then he went on to point out how it was ruining the Chinese, who drink the poisonous stuff by the tumblerful. And here is an interesting sidelight: They take brandy, he said, after their opium-smoke, to destroy the visible effects of the opium.

It seemed to me by the time they had finished that they must have unloaded enough brandy to keep the whole population of Malaya and Siam permanently intoxicated for a year. No wonder Indians and others ask me, "What is the League of Nations doing about alcohol?"

I only spent forty-eight hours in Singapore, and then caught a boat to Batavia, arriving there in the early morning of January 19th. The boat was going to Australia, a Dutch line, that starts from Singapore. Very few people were on board, and the "crossing of the line", about sunset on the 17th, passed without comment. I cannot say that it thrilled me: after all, it is, as we all learnt at school, "an invisible line," and you cannot get very excited at the sight of something you cannot see, especially when you do not really know where it is. But the tropical islets, covered in jungle, and the varying colours of the sea, really were romantic and lovely, and the sunset was one of the most beautiful I have seen. There were strange, fleecy clouds tipped with red, then turning a queer brown colour; and far above them, seemingly 50,000 feet up, wisps of cloud that kept the light very long.

It has naturally been easier for me to compare the manners of the Dutch in Java with those of the English in India, than to compare the Javanese with the Indians. On reaching Priok, the port of Batavia, you motor for several miles along a perfectly flat, straight road with a broad canal beside it, for all the world as if you were in Holland; and when you reach Weltevreden, still quite fiat, you see scores of well-fed Dutchmen dashing along the roads on their bicycles, wearing ordinary felt hats, carrying soft dispatch-cases under their arms. You see schoolboys and schoolgirls of all ages, many of them hatless, and elegant young ladies, similarly hatless, cycling about in the suburbs; just as if you were in the suburbs of The Hague. The hatlessness is the most astonishing thing; and the number of children between the ages of six and eighteen. If you ask a Dutchman about the effects of the sun, he will probably tell you that it must be more dangerous in British India, where the atmosphere is less humid, but K. A. said she had heard a great many Dutch people complain of frequent headaches, and that she had no doubt this was chiefly due to their carelessness about the sun. Of course, I think many English people in India err on the other side. I heard a story of a man who had been so careful always to wear a topee in India that when he returned to England and left it off he got a sunstroke at once. In Java I think the use of the topee is increasing.

To me the presence of schoolboys and schoolgirls was a pleasant sight; it made me realize how unnatural English society in India is without them. But, of course, many Dutch parents send their children to Holland for a few years at least. They realize the danger of allowing their children to grow up in a country where they have everything done for them by servants, and where they can order the "inferior race" to do their bidding. I sometimes wish that people could see the demoralizing effect of this environment not only on their children, but on themselves.

Perhaps they do, more often than I realize. For many I suppose the "bread and butter" argument would be their reply. Still, the number who fight against this demoralization seem to be few compared with those who justify the conquerors' attitude in themselves.

On the whole, I think the personal relationship of the Dutch to the Javanese is better than that of the British to the Indians. This is no doubt partly due to the very fact that the Dutch live a more homelike life. They have fewer furloughs and eat mostly the same food as in Holland. The business community work through the heat of the day; but otherwise the Dutch world does recognize the need for rest, and they tend to sleep from two to five. That seems to be almost the only general concession to the climate. Electric-fans are appallingly lacking. A Calvinist missionary's wife was vastly amused at my surprise at the absence of fans. In a most superior and contemptuous manner she assured me that they would never adopt such a stupid device. One of her objections was that it caused a draught. Any sane person in the Tropics sits in any draught he can find. This good lady, who has been over twenty years in the country, gave me a lot of information. Many of her statements seemed to me hardly credible, and those which I have since been able to test proved to be quite untrue! Moral: Do not believe the statements of dogmatic people.

However, this is a digression. I was writing about the relations of ruler and ruled. The position of the Eurasians is much better than in British India. An English business man told me that no white man in Java would speak disparagingly of half-castes. If you heard anyone speak that way you could be almost sure he was a half-caste himself. They are accepted in Dutch Society.

More remarkable is the fact that Dutch and Javanese "Tommies" serve together in the army and fraternize without discord. If you suggested such a possibility to a British officer in the Indian Army he would certainly have a fit!

I was interested to discover that there is a special Government department (composed of Dutch and Javanese) for keeping in touch with Javanese movements, and impressing the Government with their importance (or otherwise). At a Muslim conference that I attended at Djokja there was a special table and a few chairs set for "the authorities", next to the Press table. This is apparently a legal requirement. I sat there between Mr. P. and a Javanese, both of them members of the special department; and beyond Mr. P. sat two Dutch police officials. Mr. P., who explained the proceedings to me, is a delightful man, very liberal-minded (his name is anathema to many of the Dutch), and he seemed to be on the most friendly terms with the leaders. The discussion, which caused great excitement, was concerned with the question whether a translation of the Koran into Javanese (or Malay?) from an English translation made by Muhammad Ali could be accepted as authoritative. Of course, if the foundation of your religion is based on a verbally inspired book, such a discussion must be interesting; but I am afraid it bored me exceedingly, even though an Indian occasionally read an extract from the English translation. I thought it was rather a high testimony to the police official that, although the discussion could not conceivably have had any political significance, he seemed to follow it with the deepest interest. Perhaps he had been brought up as a strict Calvinist, and loved theological disputation as only a Dutch Calvinist can!

This is a very incoherent letter. I have been telling about a Dutch lady at Solo and a Muslim conference at Djokja, both places in mid-Java, whilst I am still on the road from Priok to Batavia. Nor have I begun to compare the Javanese and the Indians; and I can at least compare their clothes, if not their customs and their minds.

That sends me back to the Dutchmen's clothes. Most of them still wear the "old-fashioned" white coats that button right up to the neck, and they are nearly always perfectly white. And as to trousers, they *never* seem to wear shorts. In the trains everyone wears these white clothes, and as I do not like to make myself conspicuous, I have got all my suits perfectly filthy from the dirty trains, with no chance to get them washed. On the other hand, many of the men, having sweated all day in these proper clothes and probably not even taken their coats off in their office, will return home at 5 o'clock and spend the evening in pyjamas (!) until they put on another spotless white suit, all buttoned to the neck, for dinner, any time from 8 to 9.30.

I mention these things especially as they have had an appalling effect on the national costume. It would not be a serious exaggeration to say that the Javanese are a nation clad in pyjama legs; the variety of ungainly, stripey things they wear is painful to see. Some people do not like the Indian *dhoty,* but at least it has a character of its own. The Javanese pyjama is infinitely uglier; and when they get frayed at the bottom they get cut shorter and shorter, till they become long shorts flapping about the knee.

By contrast the better-class Javanese are magnificently clad. Over their trouser-legs (which may or, may not be pyjamas) they wear a splendid skirt of *batik* work, and, above it, generally a white coat buttoned up to the neck, like a Dutchman's. I wonder if this is the ancient aristocratic tunic of Java, which perhaps the first Dutch and English merchants copied in the early seventeenth century, until it became the accepted wear for Europeans in the Tropics. On their heads they wear a close-fitting turban, also with wondrous *batik* designs upon it. This alone gives them a distinguished appearance. Only the upper tenth wear any footgear, and they mostly wear sandals.

I cannot describe the women's dress. Women's dress I never did understand and never shall. But on the whole I think it is less brilliant and less graceful than in British India. Their skirts are much like the men's.

The children wear either nothing or a pair of shorts. The Indian parent begins by putting his (or her) children into a filthy shirt; the Javanese into equally untidy shorts. Of course, they may be clean and tidy when new; but, if so, they very rarely are new. There is much to be said for nakedness, but if clothing is thought more respectable I think the Javanese begin at the right end.

Well, now to get back to my narrative. I had introductions to Dr. Kraemer and Dr. van Doorn. The former is evidently a very great man in Java, a missionary who has won the respect of almost all sections of the community; but he lives at Malang in East Java, and he was exceptionally busy, before leaving for the Jerusalem Missionary Conference. So in the end I did not attempt to visit him. Dr. van Doorn lives in Weltevreden (the residential suburb of Batavia), and I went straight to his house. He took me to a convenient hotel beside the great Koningsplein, where I could wander at sunset and look at birds, and then to Dr. Slotemaker de Bruine, the missionary consul, who took me in charge and spent most of an hour telephoning to all manner of people and asking them to see me. He also took charge of my interview with the Governor-General.

The British Consul-General, with whom I dined my last evening in Java, wished me to realize that most of the Dutch people I had met were rather radical. The only deduction I could make (I am sure he did not intend me to make it) was that I had probably formed too favourable an impression of the Dutch attitude to the Javanese.

My first talk was with a Bank Director, who talked to me for an hour, took me with two of his colleagues to the business men's lunch club, and there left me in the hands of a very pleasant English business man with a long experience in Java, and evidently with knowledge of the country and its people. It seems that the business men are strongly opposed to the Government's attitude towards the Javanese. They say it is going much too fast, responding not to a real popular agitation, nor to an agitation from Moscow or Mecca, but to the foolish Radicalism of certain Government officials. It will be time enough, say the business men, to begin to talk about Javanese self-government when the Javanese begin to show some business capacity; and it is generally admitted that in that respect they are quite wanting. Apart from the European business men the middle class, the traders and shopkeepers, are practically all Chinese, who number a million in Dutch India altogether, half a million in Java: the other half-million would include a great number of plantation workers in Sumatra, Borneo, Banka, and Billiton.

But I have no doubt there is a real demand, fairly widespread, for an increasing share in government. The parties of extremists, of Communists, or of non-co-operators (following the Indian lead) are quite small. But there seems to be a growing section that believe in the political unity of Islam; and a number of moderates, including the old Javanese aristocracy, who are ready to move with the times towards a gradually developing democracy. Also there are now dozens of Javanese going to Europe for university education each year, whilst a much larger number get higher education in Java; and this has been kept up to the European standard, much more nearly than in British India. I hardly met any one who regards the influence of Moscow as serious; they seem to think that was scotched in the suppression of the rebellion last year.

At the business men's club I committed one serious *faux pas* (half on purpose, to see the effect, but I might not have done it if I had anticipated the result). I said I had been reading *Max Havelaar;* was there any truth in it? The Dutchmen looked pained; an Eurasian, who was sitting beside me, explained that the whole book was a lie, and that the author was a man of no judgment but great ambition, who was angry because he was not made Governor-General. Later I met a quiet, moderate-minded Javanese professor, who said the book did good by awakening the Dutch to their responsibilities. Perhaps one might compare its effect to that of the trial of Warren Hastings.

Others, both Dutch and English, told me that they thought *Max Havelaar* had done harm by making the Dutch very paternalistic. They insist, like the British in India, on a Prussian efficiency and meticulous attention to detail. These things are contrary to the Eastern mind and cause resentment. Western administrators in the East certainly seem to be between the devil and the deep sea. If they conform to custom we abuse them for lowering their standards of justice and integrity; if they act as Western administrators they alienate their Eastern subjects. But sympathy and imagination can build bridges. Mr. P., of the Bureau for Native Affairs, has both qualities, and those Dutch in Java who are deficient hate him accordingly.

Mr. P. put me in touch with a very clever little man, Hajee Salim, not a Javanese, but I think from Sumatra, whose ability is generally recognized. What he said carried a good deal of force while you listened, but somehow it lost its force when you were away. The chief things he argued when I visited him were the inevitable tendency of the East to do its trading without the assistance of London and Amsterdam; and the menace of the Nordic superiority cult of America, which he seemed to think expressed the whole mind of the supposedly Christian West. I advised him to read Oldham's book, with its complete destruction of the popular pseudo-scientific poison of Stoddart. Why is it that the East gets hold of the worst of the West and thinks that worst representative?

Salim is vice-president of the rather small Sareka Islam party who called the conference at Djokja and who champion the translation of the Koran. I noticed that his interventions at Djokja were very coldly received. The president, who seemed to be a kind of De Valera, made hot, emotional speeches that roused the enthusiasm of a section; but those who applauded Salim were a mere handful. Apparently he is not trusted. He has the brains, but it is doubtful if he has much else. He and his friends seemed to be fighting a losing battle over the Koran. Most of the other Javanese leaders speak no English.

The head of the Chinese section and a German missionary who has lived in China gave me two different and complementary accounts of the Chinese in Java. A great many of the locally born Chinese do not speak Chinese at all; they only use Malay, which is the *lingua franca* of this part of the world. One of my fellow passengers on the boat from Colombo to Penang argued that it would be far better than English, French, or Esperanto as the universal language: it is very easy to learn. But to learn well?—I doubt it. Many Chinese in Java, of course, also learn Dutch. There is a considerable mixed population, as many of the early immigrants married Dutch wives.

Family life is the basis of everything for the Chinese. Until lately they have paid very little attention to local politics. But the interest is increasing. They now have five representatives in the Volksraad.

The local Chinese seem to care little for the current politics of China; but the large number of immigrants, who are recruited for a year or eighteen months to work on estates or in tin mines, are mostly ardent members of the Kuomintang. But even in its Communist days they were not real Communists; they tend to explain away the Communist teachings of Sun Yat Sen.

The local Chinese are a prosperous and growing community, with their own schools. Each year about eight new Chinese schools are opened. The German missionary told me an amusing tale. One day lately he was talking to an old Chinese shopkeeper. He happened to reveal that he was not a Dutchman. "Are you an Englishman?"—No. "An American?"—No. When he found he was a German, he said, "Ah then, if you are a German, I can tell you a secret. In forty years' time this country will not belong to the Dutch; it will belong to the Chinese." Whether that was an individual idiosyncrasy or the expression of a widespread secret purpose, I cannot judge.

Many of the Chinese smoke opium. The majority learn the habit in *Insulinde*. Amongst the leading Chinese there is a strong anti-opium opinion, but they have not yet been very successful in turning opinion into action. Probably it is not easy, in view of Government policy. The acting head of the opium *regie* told me a good deal less than he might; he did not tell me that his chief was just returning from a journey to Persia and Turkey to negotiate for opium to take the place of the reduced Indian supply. That I only learnt from quite another quarter, three hours before my boat left Batavia and so too late to see the returned chief. Nor did he suggest my visiting the opium factory in Batavia. I did not even know there was one, though I suppose I ought to have done. But by good luck I found that two young Americans who are on this boat had come upon this factory by chance yesterday morning, and had spent an hour seeing over it; and some of the things they have told me are curious and rather puzzling. I fear the Dutch opium policy is subtler than I had thought.

The Professor of International Law, Baron van Asbeck, explained to me the position of the Javanese territories that are under the personal rule of "Regents" or "Sultans"—Javanese aristocrats or ancient hereditary rulers whose position is roughly comparable to some of the second-class Indian princes. The

Dutch Government hold that international obligations are of paramount importance. Therefore, if at Geneva the Dutch Government, representing all the Dutch Indies, agrees to suppress opium or to improve labour conditions, the Regents must carry out these agreements in their territories. The treaties by which the Dutch Government is bound to them are of inferior status to international conventions; and therefore, if there is any seeming conflict, the international convention must be respected. This doctrine certainly tends to enhance the position of international law. I am afraid it will be a long time before the Great Powers will agree that an international convention should have superior validity to a municipal law. But this Dutch doctrine may have some application to the relationship of British India and the Indian States.

Another interesting talk was with the Vice-President of the Volksraad, a Javanese aristocrat, the Ario Adipatti Soemoedo Joedo (Eng. pron., *Soomoodo Yoodo)*. He thinks the Government is moving at about the right pace, in keeping with the growth of national feeling. Democracy is not in accordance with Javanese tradition, but it is in the air to-day, and so its forms must be to a large extent adopted. But the vital question seems to be the proper education of the country. On this I got the views of two or three leading Javanese as well as Dutch. Hitherto the system has been too Dutch, too Western; but how is that to be amended? Before the Dutch came a few administrators had a literary education, there were Muslim schools for teaching the Koran, and girls learnt *batik* and other handicraft; and that was all. Can the history of the world and the science of the West be combinded with a training in essentially Javanese arts and crafts? And if that is done, how will it affect the political outlook of the people?

Another Javanese I met, a Christian schoolmaster with a very fine school in Weltevreden, also spoke of the need for making education less literary. The Governor-General himself, with whom I had a ten minutes' interview, emphasized the same thing. The Governor-General received me simply and kindly. He knew of Woodbrooke and said it had a high reputation in Holland, intimating that he shared that opinion. I could not help being amused at the thought that this Dutch statesman, ruler of this great Eastern empire, knew of Woodbrooke, whilst Sir Austen Chamberlain, the life-long inhabitant of Birmingham, when I saw him last year, had never heard of the place. I must not record the private conversation of a man in such a responsible position; but I can, at least, say that he impressed me as a man of liberal and humane outlook, open to reasonable suggestions from any quarter, and sincerely concerned for the welfare of all the inhabitants of this heterogeneous empire. He has many critics, but I think he is strong enough to take his own line, and even to adopt from his critics any proposal that may have real value. He remonstrated at the shortness of my visit, and pointed to the danger of making comparisons with British India.

I had had a very warm invitation from K. A. to stay with her Dutch husband and herself at Tjiandjoer, a little town in the mountains, a few hours by train from Batavia. Thither I went as soon as I could leave Batavia, eager in this remote land to get to some place where I could talk about home. They were most kind, and knew just what a tired traveller wanted to make him really comfortable. They have been in Java nearly two years, at Tjiandjoer nearly one. They have evidently not spared themselves in learning the language: it is Sundanese there; Javanese is the language of mid- and east Java. It sounds an alarming sort of language. It has three different forms (or more), according to whether you are addressing your superiors, your equals, or your inferiors; and you have to be very careful which form you use. They pointed out one result of this. The man who translated the New Testament into Sundanese assumed that Jesus, being God, should always be made to speak in the language used to inferiors. B. and K. A., of course, think that this gives the people a totally false idea of Christ and of his Gospel. Their house is just an ordinary Sundanese house, built on bamboos, with a stone veranda in front; their landlord is a pleasant young Javanese, who, like other property-owners, suffers from lack of any useful occupation. For some time before they came there had been no missionary in Tjiandjoer.

There is a small Christian community—Christian by tradition rather than by life. They confessed it might be almost easier for them if there were no Christians at all. But that and all other difficulties I feel sure they will overcome. They seem to be on the friendliest terms with all the people of the place, including the leading people, from the Regent downwards.

In Tjiandjoer, as in other parts of Java, there is at present a great demand among the aristocracy and the intellectuals to learn English; and this is strongly encouraged by the authorities. The A.s are receiving many requests from people who want to learn English. Two more such requests came while I was there, and they hardly knew whether they could give more lessons. They all offer good fees; these the A.s refuse, but the fees go to some charity. The Regent's wife is one of K. A.'s pupils.

B. A. gives lessons to the Patti, who is the chief man after the Regent; and to the head of the chief local school. All these people are Muslims, of course. One day I came in while he was giving the schoolmaster his lesson, and at the end of it we had a friendly talk. He struck me as a fine man. When he had gone I noticed a copy of the Gospel of John lying on the table. This puzzled me, as I felt sure he was a Muslim. I said nothing, but a few minutes later the mystery was revealed. B. A. told me quite simply, and as if it were the most natural proceeding, that he had been getting the schoolmaster's help with his sermon for Sunday, and that he had been very helpful in explaining what phrases and ideas that B. had proposed using were foreign to the mentality of the people. The picture of this Muslim schoolmaster helping the Christian missionary to prepare his sermon seems to me to be the most perfect example of the working of the real Christian spirit that I have met on my travels. I do not prophesy any wonderful number of "conversions" in Tjiandjoer; but while the A.s are there I do not see how the Christian spirit can help growing and flourishing.

Monday was the Chinese New Year's Day; and we woke up early to the noise of a tremendous bombardment of crackers. We had a pleasant little walk through the woods to the roaring Tjiandjoer river, which comes tumbling down from the great

10,000-foot volcano, some 15 miles from the town. Later in the day I went with B. A. to meet three of his English pupils, three youths, one of them being his landlord. Instead of the usual English lesson I told them about the Indian National Congress, B. A. translating. I tried to speak slowly and distinctly, and they said they understood a good deal without the translation. I did not feel quite clear what effect my account of the Congress might have upon them—whether it would rouse their national emotions or lead them to think that what was said by Indian leaders was true for Java. But who was I to act the political censor? B. A. felt sure that it would interest them, that they would discuss it for days, so I gladly did what he proposed. When we suggested that they might like to ask some questions, one of them asked if I thought Mr. Gandhi was a chameleon—always changing his colour, as he had seen suggested somewhere. I energetically combated the suggestion, but I could not help approving of the proper critical mind of the youth that seemed to prompt the question.

In the evening we went to see some Javanese dancing at the Regent's. The Patti had kindly persuaded three friends of his, all expert Javanese dancers, to perform for our benefit. Each man in turn did one complete dance. The lady who acted as their foil was not so expert. Both the music and the dancing were amazing and very weird. The more refined the dancer is the less he "dances" in our Western sense. It is all a question of subtle rhythmical movements of the joints, especially fingers, elbows, and knees. Most Javanese are said to be double-jointed (also babies born in Java: the A. baby, so his mother told me, has double-jointed fingers). Each dance represents a story known to the Javanese audience, and they get greatly excited as the story develops. Unfortunately I do not know the names of the instruments that composed the band (except drums); but the sound is rather nearer our music than Indian music is. The players on the Regent's instruments were the most marvellous collection of human figures: I found them almost more fascinating than the dancers. They looked as if they had all come straight out of one of Shakespeare's low-life scenes.

I went on from Tjiandjoer to Bandoeng. When first I travelled in India I was horrified at the seeming wastefulness of the cultivation. In Java I was greatly struck, on the other hand, by the ingenuity of the peasants, especially in the construction of their rice-fields on steep hill-sides or even mountain slopes. The banking up and irrigation of the terraced rice-fields is marvellous. I cannot think how they do it. Sometimes the banks are two or three feet high; and a bank of that height may be made to hold a field that is less than half an acre in size. And so on all up the hill-side; and every field holding water. Of course, this is the rainy season, and there are usually heavy storms each afternoon; still, the success of the whole thing is really marvellous. They get three rice crops in the year in some places. The method is said to have been brought from India; so we must give India her due. From Buitenzorg to Tjiandjoer and on to Bandoeng is all mountainous country, and certainly beautifully green and luxuriant and in places magnificent; but I do not know why Java should be called the earthly paradise. That is not in the tropics at all; it is off the north-west coast of Europe. Nature is altogether too violent in the Tropics; it knows nothing of the gentle modulations and quiet contours and soft colours and cool, invigorating winds of England. And I do not think Paradise is a place where you are in a beastly sweat all the time—even when you lie down on your bed. Oh yes, that reminds me of another curious Dutch habit. When you go to bed in Java you find nothing on your bed but a sheet to lie on, a couple of magnificent Dutch pillows for your head, and a bolster down the middle of the bed. Now, I rather like some covering over me at night, even in the Tropics. Otherwise I do not feel as if I was really "in bed". But what to do with that bolster? I have never discovered. B. A., Junior, who had two baby bolsters, had adopted the left-hand one as a favourite doll; and his mother was just giving it eyes, nose, and mouth, to his gurgling delight. But they really cannot expect grown-up people to want dolls to play with at night. What is that bolster for?

I saw no wild animals in Java, except one; though along the little-known south coast there are apparently fierce beasts of various kinds, including a great black sort of cattle; they are said to have a habit, on seeing a man, not of charging straight, but coming round behind and charging him in the back. Very unsporting. The one "wild animal" I saw was a brown monkey. Really I cannot regard monkeys as wild animals; they are so plainly semi-human. The sight I had of this one was very odd. I saw it from the train. We were going along beside a channel, with jungly vegetation beyond. Suddenly I saw the top part of a rotten stump break off and fall into the water, and the next moment a monkey appeared out of the water, looking perfectly composed, pretending that nothing had happened at all; and proceeded (apparently, but by that time it was lost to sight) to climb back on to the rotten stump which had so rudely thrown it into the water just as the train came by.

Bandoeng is a comparatively cool place; the Dutch military and some other departments are making it their headquarters. It would be a suitable place, I should think, for the capital. It is four hours by the direct train from Batavia. Its one natural drawback is that the water is horribly sulphurous and smelly. There are all sorts of exciting volcanic activities near it, but I had neither time nor money to visit them.

I had good talks with two doctors of the mission hospital, who are treating opium addicts. One or two unsuccessful attempts to cure opium-smokers by hospital treatment have been made in Java in the recent past; now they have learned the necessary conditions of permanent success and are doing much better. They were most anxious to be told about opium conditions in India, and I found I was giving more information than I got!

It was a long journey to Djokja, in mid-Java. Besides the Muslim Conference I saw the mission schools and hospital—a very finely equipped, new group of buildings; and a Javanese school, started six or seven years ago, whose founder owes his inspiration to Montessori and Tagore. I certainly felt something of the Santiniketan spirit there. The little children sit on the floor as they do in their homes; they repeat their lessons in chorus—a thing Eastern children seem to appreciate; they do it with zest. They sang some of their songs. This they do twice a week. Much use is made of ancient Javanese folklore in the teaching. Teachers and children make a happy family. Finally the "band" performed, and made a glorious din. I am afraid the kind missionary who gave up a good deal of his morning to me was not unnaturally a little bored that I was more interested in this than in the very proper schools of the mission.

From Djokja I visited Borobudur. If I did not appreciate this extraordinary Buddhist ruin as much as I ought, at any rate I spent a peaceful afternoon and saw a lot of birds. I had a curious experience as I was standing close under the top *stupa,* when I suddenly heard a strange, tapping noise that seemed to come from inside the stupa, and a moment later a great Death's Head Hawk moth came dashing past the top of the *stupa* and settled suddenly among the stones just in front of my feet.

I also spent one night and part of a day at Solo.

The people of Java are nearly all nominally Muslims, but in mid-Java the Muslim influence is very slight, and farther east it hardly exists. I saw scarcely anything in Java, outside the Sareka Islam Conference, that was typical of the influence Islam generally has over its members. I saw neither the regular devotions nor the orderly democratic feeling, nor any of the harsher Muslim characteristics. I suspect that the people are still closer to the Hindus in life and thought than to the full-blooded Muslims of North India and the Middle East. Their culture is, of course, notoriously Hindu in origin; the *batik* work, the puppet-shows and drama, are derived from the *Ramayana* and the *Mahabharata.*

In such a situation a prosperous Christian mission can achieve prodigies in the way of "conversions". The Calvinist missionaries in mid-Java are more successful in adding to the number of Christian members than, I believe, any other missionaries who work among Muslims. I wonder what it all amounts to. I dare say they are getting educated; but whether the education they are getting is the kind they really need I could not feel sure. Also they are getting good medical assistance. That is an undoubted benefit. But I doubt if they are better men and women after their baptism than before.

K. A. told me that two "Christian" girls at Tjiandjoer, converted under an earlier dispensation, though working together, never seemed to have any thought of helping each other. When she suggested that Christians ought to help one another, they gaped in amazement at such a notion. No wonder Mr. Gandhi says conversion encourages hypocrisy. I met one truly humble-minded servant of Christ at Solo; and the head-mistress of the girls' school seemed to be one who had a teacher's instinct, loving her flock and making them a happy family. Yet I left mid-Java with a heavy heart. As in India I had seen *sadhus* bring the Hindu religion into derision; as at Darjeeling the fat and flourishing priests mocked the memory of the gentle Gautama; so here I seemed to see how success turns the Christian missionary from humble service to proud domination. In India the same thing can be found: ambassadors of Christ who are doing their master the greatest disservice. They have forgotten the one thing needful.

Mid-Java is said to be much more backward than west Java. The Sultan there still has much power; the population is very dense; the women are made to do most of the work. Most of the land is held by Western companies, who grow sugar-cane, bananas, and other things to sell in the West. There is a good deal of nationalist criticism of this; but a Batavia professor, whose authority I am inclined to accept, assured me that if rice were grown instead half the people would starve. The high prices paid abroad for the sugar, etc., enable the workers to get sufficiently good wages to buy imported rice and other necessities.

All the people I saw in Java looked better fed and more prosperous than India's underfed millions. Generally speaking, they have much better houses.

Compared with the Indians, I think the Javanese are an unsophisticated, gay, happy-go-lucky-people. When you arrive at a railway station a couple of coolies will seize your luggage and dash off without the least idea where you are going; and when you have got your ticket and paid for your heavy luggage they have totally vanished. Presently they reappear from some remote end of the wrong platform, full of laughter and gaiety, as if it were all the best joke on earth. I can well believe that they spend all their money as soon as they get it. As in India, the small boys have a splendid time looking after the water-buffaloes, swimming after them, riding on their backs, washing them, and keeping the great quiet beasts in order. One day I saw a big youth in the street suddenly catch hold of his little brother's foot and kiss his leg, apparently out of sheer elder-brotherly emotion. I think they live very much in the present. Perhaps all unsophisticated people do. One day, as my taxi was dashing round a corner in Weltevreden it came into my mind that probably my driver would be quite as content to be killed in a glorious smash at that moment as to live through a number of years each one rather less exciting and more painful. And I wondered if there were any good reason why I should care more for the continuance of my life than he did for his. I cautiously concluded that perhaps there was; and he kindly allowed me to continue it.

VIII

On The Sea Between Penang And Rangoon,
February 19th

The other day an American lady missionary told me that folk in America seemed rather doubtful whether Singapore was in China or India; but they were sure it must be in one or the other. And a lady in Java, when I asked her if she had been in British India, replied, "Oh yes, I have been at Colombo and at Singapore and at Hong-Kong."

But, all the same, Malaya really is the place where China and India meet. Until 1867, I think, the British possessions here, the so-called Straits Settlements, were under the East India Company; and old maps show the whole peninsula as "Farther India". On the other hand, for four hundred years or so Malaya has been colonized by the Chinese; and to-day they form two-thirds of the population of Singapore and the backbone of all the towns in the country. From the other side thousands of Tamil labourers from South India come and work on the rubber estates and in the tin mines. As you travel through the country by train or motor-car you see Chinese everywhere and Indians nearly everywhere, and you begin to wonder where on earth the Malays can be. The explanation is that most Malays live by the rivers, and they do not take much part in the development of the country. I have seen very little of them, so what I have learned of them has nearly all been at second hand. They are, of course, closely akin to the Javanese and the other inhabitants of the chief Dutch East Indies. Indeed, it is a little awkward to know what words to use: Malay means the whole "Malay" race, including Sundanese and Javanese, and the inhabitants of Sumatra, Borneo, and other islands, as well as the Malay

Peninsula. Sundanese can also be used for the whole race. But "Malay" is also used in a more restricted sense as the "Malay" inhabitants of the peninsula. A further complication arises from the fact that a good number of the present inhabitants of Malaya are recent immigrants from Sumatra or Java.

The Malays seem to live a placid, unambitious life. They live in scattered villages called *kampongs,* clearings in the jungle near the rivers, where they grow a little rice communally, and some coco-nut palms, bananas, and a few other foodstuffs; they also fish. A good many of them have shown capacity as mechanics, motor-drivers, sea captains, and in various crafts; but a Malayan merchant, or a Malayan rubber-planter or tin-miner, is almost or quite unknown. The Government has lately assigned certain forest areas near the Malay Settlements or along the rivers as Malay reservations, so that they shall not be utterly squeezed out by the more vigorous races. These reservations seem likely to remain largely unused for some time to come; yet their area is relatively small. Some people think the Malays are a dying race—that they will gradually disappear under the pressure of their neighbours, especially the Chinese.

I have begun with the Malays because the country is called Malaya. But even the Malays are comparatively recent inhabitants. In the jungles on the hills there are primitive people called Sacci and others. I saw very few of these. Some diving boys at Singapore belonged to an aboriginal fishing people. But that sends me back farther still to the geography and topography of the country. I had better say something about the environment; I can come back to human beings later.

Malaya is about the size of England, 450 miles from end to end, 200 miles across. The mail train takes nearly twenty-four hours from Singapore to Penang, less than 400 miles. Singapore Island, which is the same size and shape as the Isle of Wight, is rather flat, with no high hills; so is a good deal of Johare, the southernmost State. And there is a low-lying stretch of country along the south-west and west to within 50 or 100 miles of Penang. Above this, a good deal nearer the west than the east coast, runs a long chain of mountains, rising to 7,000 or 8,000 feet in a few places, and mostly over 4,000 along the central ridges. To the east of this the country gradually descends to the China Sea. There are further hill ranges to the north-west of the country, the hill on Penang Island itself rising to 2,700 feet. I have not seen the eastern side of the main range at all; but I believe it is mostly uncultivated virgin jungle. The main range of hills, as seen from the west, is entirely covered with jungle. I suppose a hundred years ago at least nine-tenths of the whole country were under dense jungle.

The jungle contains an immense variety of trees. Over twelve hundred species are known, which is a larger number than all the species found in India. Many of the forest trees grow straight up for 50 or 100 feet before they have any branches. So, unless he has the luck to find one that has just fallen, the botanist must have some difficulty in "collecting" specimens. They are practically all evergreen. The ground in the jungle is so dark and damp that fallen trees rot away in a few months. Mostly their wood is very soft and useless to man. My best jungle walk was on the chief hill, Bukit Timah, on Singapore Island, with H., of the Botanic Gardens. At one place we came upon what looked like a giant mole-run. I asked H. what it was. He said it was the remains of a fallen tree-trunk; and within the next half-hour we saw several more in rather earlier stages of decay. The rapidity of growth is equally remarkable. Some of the bamboos grow six inches in one day.

The jungle is not all composed of giant trees. Beneath these are many smaller trees, and there are many different kinds of creeper, with great festoons or roots hanging from the branches of the big trees, and immense quantities of ferns, from tiny lichen-like things that grow on rocks or tree-trunks, to tall tree-ferns in the hills. Many of the big trees (a number of which belong to the fig tribe) have ferns and other plants growing on them; most of these are not parasites but epiphytes: that is, they do not get their sustenance from their host, but they collect it themselves from the air and the rain.

We spotted a fine red-flowered rhododendron growing as an epiphyte on one of the big trees in the Singapore jungle. The

East Himalayas and West China mountains are the great haunt of rhododendrons; but a few occur on the hills right down through Burma and Malaya, and, I believe, in the higher mountains of Borneo and Sumatra.

Flowers are astonishingly few. There is an occasional tree with bright red or violet or yellow flowers; but the jungle as a whole is monotonously green. English people get weary of the perpetual unchanging green. Small flowering plants are still more scarce. Most of the trees are rather uninteresting and undistinguished. I several times noticed one, not a big tree, with a huge "oak" leaf three or four feet long. I didn't discover its name. Most of the trees seem to have ordinary little round leaves, and few have dense foliage. There is too much competition for space and air to give any one tree much of a chance. A few species have big juicy fruits, but Europeans do not seem to appreciate their taste as much as the Malays do.

To atone for the absence of flowers the Malayan jungle is very rich in butterflies. I have been seeing gorgeous butterflies everywhere since I first reached India, but the butterflies of the Malayan jungle surpass all the others, alike in size, variety, and brilliance of colouring. How they manage with so few flowers I cannot think; but at least they atone for the lack of flowers. Some of the Malayan butterflies, I understand, would be worth £10 in Europe. If that is so, they must be worth at least £100 flying wild in their natural haunts.

Outside the jungle most of the land to-day is under rubber. The original "india-rubber" came from certain kinds of fig *(ficus)*, which are still common in these jungles. But the rubber-tree of to-day is a native of Brazil. I believe about fifty years ago a dozen seeds were smuggled out of Brazil to Kew Gardens, and rubber-trees were grown there. Seeds from Kew were brought to Malaya, so the millions of rubber-trees here to-day are all descended from those smuggled seeds. To-day the seed is so common that labourers have to go round at this time of year pulling up the little rubber jungles that are springing up in the plantations. The rubber is not an exciting tree. Its one claim to merit in this part of the world is that it is deciduous. Just at this time of year many of the trees are a beautiful gold or red, and others quite leafless.

Then in some places, especially at Penang, you see patches of palm-tree, even great groves of palms. Penang takes its name from one of the many local species.

Finally, as you cross the country by rail or road, you come from time to time to open desolations, in some cases largely flooded, with huge engines—dredgers—squatting about in their midst, or with tall scaffoldings and ugly sheds, and gashes or quarries in the ground. These are tin mines. They suggest the "blasted heath" of Macbeth, where the witches danced. Here the only witches seem to be nightjars, which make a wearisome tapping noise, as of a nail being hammered into wood, through the night. They are known as "coffin birds".

The tin seems mostly to be found where the limestone and igneous rocks come close together. The low country is chiefly limestone, the hills are igneous. Although a great belt of volcanic islands, from Japan through the Philippines and Java and Sumatra, stretches all round, there is no evidence of recent volcanic action in Malaya, and they get no earthquakes. But there are certain geological mysteries. Near Kuala Lumpur I saw some hot springs—too hot to put your hand in; columns of steam rise high into the air from them. Now, I understand that such hot springs are usually found in the neighbourhood of active volcanoes, or, if not, that they are very impure, being contaminated by the long series of strata through which they have passed. But this water is quite good to drink.

Then, between Ipoh and Taiping, there are great limestone cliffs, solid blocks of limestone, 150 feet high, and two or three miles long, standing on top of the rest of the limestone; at the base they have caves, apparently made by sea waves long ago. How did these great blocks come to be there? A borer (a man employed by tin companies to bore for tin), whom I met at Ipoh, told me that each geologist who comes to the country propounds some new theory to account for them.

So much for the country. Now for people and politics.

The political arrangements of the country are complicated. There are the Straits Settlements, the Federated Malay States, and the Unfederated Malay States. The first are British possessions, the second under British Protectorate, the third less closely connected with Britain by treaty. The Straits Settlements are four (not including certain territories in Borneo and other remote islands). First there is Penang Island, which has been British since the eighteenth century, and opposite it Wellesley Province. The British authorities apparently still pay quite a large annual "rent", or tribute, to the Sultan of Kedah (short *e)* for this territory. Then in the south there is Singapore Island, whose important position and possibilities were recognized by Raffles in 1819. Since then two other coastal strips—Malacca, formerly Dutch, and the Dindings—have been annexed. Then, during the nineteenth century, the Sultans of Perak, Pahang, Negri-Sembilan and Selangor all accepted British "protection"; and I can quite well believe that they would have been worse off without it—or at least that their Malay population would have been. For the alternative would have been an unregulated exploitation of the country by Europeans and Chinese for its tin, and later for rubber and other plantations. But to-day the protectorate is practically equivalent to annexation. The Sultans have no power and little property. They no longer sit in the Federal Council, though they are represented there. Decisions of the Government are submitted to them, I believe, for approval. But their agreement is a mere formality. It would probably be well economically if these States could be administered along with the Straits Settlements. But that will never happen, I suppose, as international propriety forbids annexation to-day, and the de-annexation of the Straits Settlements seems unlikely.

The Unfederated States—four in number—are comparatively undeveloped. The British advisers only advise. The Sultans rule, and the administration is in the hands of Malays; this means comparative inefficiency and corruption, but that is quite understood, and probably better liked than the cold efficiency of the British. A British official who has just been visiting some of these territories told me yesterday of a British adviser who interfered so much that he doubled the revenue in one year; then he was removed, as the Royal Family of the Sultan complained that they were all starving! Johore is the most important of the Unfederated States. It covers the southern end of the peninsula, and much rubber is cultivated there. The Sultan is said to be very rich.

Malaya to-day means tin and rubber. It produces more than half the world's supply of tin, and a considerable proportion of the world's rubber. As the Straits Settlements contain the chief ports and nearly all the trading interest, the Federated States depend quite alarmingly for their prosperity on the market value of these two commodities. Recently, as a result of the activities of a financial ring in London, the price of tin fell from £308 per ton to £235, or something like that. Against such manipulations of the world market prices the people of Malaya are at present powerless to protect themselves. I cannot think that such methods of playing with the prosperity of millions ought to be possible.

Still, Malaya is a very rich country. Some twenty or thirty millions of dollars (1 Straits dollar equals 2s. 4d.) were recently spent on a futile attempt to make a new harbour on the coast opposite Penang. The money was all wasted, but the country is not languishing under the catastrophe. There is no income tax. But a good deal of revenue comes from opium and other "vices"—in the Straits Settlements over half the revenue, in the F.M.S. I think nearly a third. The rest comes from tin and rubber.

So long as the country remains prosperous the various communities—Chinese, Indian, Malay, and European—seem to live quite contentedly side by side. What might happen in adversity I do not know. They import most of their rice from Siam, and once during the war it nearly gave out. It is really impressive to see the races mingling so happily, though each community lives mainly to itself, and the Europeans suffer from the usual "superiority complex" of the white man. I fancy that the Chinese also regard all the other races, or at least the Europeans, with silent contempt.

I seem to have committed myself to a lot of second-hand generalities. I hope they are not very inaccurate. Anyhow, I think my tendency is usually to underestimate rather than to exaggerate. Well, now for the things I have myself seen and heard. I had several hours on shore at Penang as long ago as January 13th. Immediately I discovered that I was in China, or at least a Chinese colony. The shops had Chinese inscriptions; some of the streets were hung all along with Chinese signs. The coolies were all carrying things on their shoulders (or rather on one shoulder), suspended from the two ends of a bamboo, instead of carrying them on their heads. And the weights they carry are amazing. They never wear a pad, and yet you never see a sore shoulder—at least, I never did. The development of the shoulder muscles is tremendous. Their faces are far more impassive and inscrutable than those of the Indians. One day in Java I was travelling opposite a Chinese father and his little girl, aged perhaps two or three. The little girl was absolutely impassive, and refused to smile, even when her father became friendly and smiled.

I suppose it would not be fair to judge China from the Chinese of Malaya any more than you could judge England from Australia or South Africa. But I must say the contrast with India is very acute. The whole country is bent on getting rich quickly, and the Chinese certainly lead in the race. Nearly all the big houses of Penang and Singapore and Kuala Lumpur have Chinese names advertised on their gates, and the tawdriness of the display is not pleasing. Many of the Straits Chinese appear to be as vulgar as the *nouveaux riches* of Europe. They have "made the country", and they are still making it, and they intend the fact to be known.

In my two days at Singapore, before leaving for Java, I did not do very much. But I visited the League of Nations Far Eastern Epidemiological Bureau, and in the absence of his chief the deputy, a Pole with a German name—Deutschmann, in fact—explained the work they are doing, and the marvellous diagrams on the walls showing the various categories of the health arrangements at the ports, and where the weekly wireless reports are distributed from Madagascar and Kenya and the Persian Gulf to Japan and the Philippines and Australia: at present plague, cholera, and smallpox are the three diseases on which they concentrate. India seems to be co-operating rather less than one could wish.

I. H., who was temporarily working with the Y.W.C.A. at Singapore, asked me if I would speak at the Y.W.C.A. on "The League of Nations" when I returned; and I agreed to do so. The meeting was held under the auspices of the International Fellowship, whose chairman is an Indian judge, an old Cambridge man. It was a remarkably interesting and difficult audience to address: there were Chinese, Indians, Japanese, Americans, Arabs, Malays, and various Europeans—a typical Singapore audience. I was also rather embarrassed by the arrival of the head of the Epidemiological Bureau, a French-Swiss doctor who has been on the Secretariat at Geneva for some years. I guessed he had come to find who this fellow could be who ventured to talk about the League. But I had some pleasant talk with him before the meeting began, and of course I referred to his presence at the beginning. I took the line of regarding the League in its historic setting as an important step in the inevitable development of international co-operation following the revolution in communications. And I illustrated this by discussing international health work, drug restrictions, labour regulations, and other things of local interest. I only referred to the League's political achievements at the end, partly to explain why it was preoccupied at the moment with European problems—clearing up the mess left in Europe by the war. Asia's contribution to the League was bound to become increasingly important.

The real representative of the League, who explained the work of the Far Eastern Bureau before the end of the meeting, seemed satisfied, which was a comfort.

After the meeting I had interesting talks with a number of people, especially with a Chinese Christian doctor, Chen Su Lan, who has had many years' experience among Chinese of all classes, and who offered to tell me all about opium, and to take me to an opium den on the following day; which he did.

The opium den was a depressing place. It was far cleaner and more airy and spacious than the Calcutta dens, but the smokers were quite young men, most of them smoking just for fun, or to discuss their business together, but two, at least, rather older, completely captured and ruined by the drug. Government has control of all opium retail shops and smoking dens now, but there is no restriction of the amount sold, except that only Chinese may buy it. The doctor assured me that nearly all those who take to opium gradually require more and more. Other Chinese have told me the same. English officials, on the other hand, say that the Chinese take a fixed amount, and that the great majority are, and remain, moderate smokers. It is not easy to get at the truth.

During my visits to Singapore I stayed with R. E. H. and his wife at the Botanic Gardens. It is a beautiful place, and I was constantly hearing the note of some bird or other that I wanted to see. During the afternoon usually a large tribe of monkeys would appear in the trees and on the grass near the house. They were particularly fond of a huge festoon by which they could climb across from one large tree to another; on this natural swing they would sit, one above the other, and play the vulgar game of "Scratch my back for fleas and I'll scratch yours". The said fleas (if fleas they are) are devoured with much satisfaction. One day, as we came up the garden, a certain monkey was sitting on the grass, obviously refusing to be disturbed by the appearance of his upright cousins. I suddenly turned my binoculars on to him. He still pretended indifference, but then he happened conveniently to remember an important appointment with a lady in the trees, and quietly turned and marched off in perfect order.

The H's. took me several pleasant motor-rides after tea; one day we went to see the Naval Base. I was assured there was nothing to see. However, I thought I ought to see it! "Nothing" very nearly expresses it. From a small jetty we saw the half-dozen little tugs that are at work. I believe the dredger is at present out of order. It is a beautiful spot—the strait between the island and Johore is here about a mile wide; both sides are lined with jungle. Close to the famous Base a common sandpiper and two white-collared kingfishers were sitting on the mud; and we watched two flying lizards on the trunks of some palm-trees. The Naval Base apparently requires a Flying Base to support it; this is being made a few miles off. One of the few remaining bits of real jungle on Singapore Island is being destroyed to make it, and C., of the Museum, lamented that he was receiving from the men who are at work there specimens of rare animals which will probably never be seen alive on Singapore again. So the militarists have begun to take their toll of irreplaceable life already.

I left Singapore by the night mail for Kuala Lumpur on the evening of February 6th, reaching K.L. (as it is commonly called—the capital of the F.M.S.) early on the 7th. At K.L. I was kindly entertained by a Socialist lawyer who assisted my father in his anti-opium work twenty years ago. He introduced me to the leading members of the Indian Association, and they very kindly entertained me to lunch. One of them, Mr. Veeraswamy, has just been appointed a member of the Federal Council—he is the first Indian member. I thought him a fine man, a real Indian. I also met the representative in Malaya of the Government of India: he also is an Indian. He looks after the interests of the Indian immigrants. There were also Indian doctors and lawyers, a business man who has close connections with a Birmingham firm, and the one and only Indian who runs a tin-mine. My first afternoon at K.L. we visited a tin-mine with its manager. Conditions of labour appear to be good for the East.

One morning I saw Harrisons, Barker's Seaport rubber estate, a few miles out. The factory seemed to be a pleasant place to work in; the local manager seemed to be on easy terms with the workers, and the lines (where the coolies live) are better than the average. There was a pleasant school, where the children can stay as long as they like; a delightful crêche with a nurse in attendance, and an airy hospital. There were only two or three slight malaria cases at the moment, but one man was in hospital, partly paralysed; he has no relations in India to whom he can be sent, so he is apparently being kept by the firm in hospital—for the rest of his natural life? It happens that there is an Unemployment

Insurance measure before the Federal Council just now. It has been a good deal delayed. In my presence F. discussed it with the Labour Minister (if that is his title). There seems to be nothing now to prevent its enactment; but another question or two may be necessary in Parliament to prevent the Colonial Office going to sleep. Education of the children of the plantation coolies is now practically compulsory. The State contributes part of the cost. There are some Chinese employed on Harrisons, Barker's estates as well as Indians; and I found the same in the tin mines; they apparently work quite happily side by side. They live in separate lines. The manager explained to me that if they keep some Chinese, then in case of a sudden demand for rubber they have a good chance to get extra labour, recruiting fresh labour in India is a much slower and more difficult undertaking. For some Chinese labourers are now settling permanently in Malaya; the Indians mostly return to India—the home pull is stronger. The Chinese carry their households and their household gods with them; the Indians may bring their families, but their religion binds them to India. One of the opium officials at K.L. showed me over the opium factory, and took me to an opium den and a retail shop. The number of 3-hoon packets—enough for a normal daily consumption—prepared each day is prodigious.

After two days at Kuala Lumpur I took the train north again, as far as Tanjong Malim, on the border of Selangor and Perak. Here E.M., who is health inspector for one of the districts of Perak, met me, and he took me to see a Malay teachers' training school and a small mission school before motoring me through some beautiful country to his home at Tapah, where it was very delightful to have a couple of days with him and his wife. But I must give some account of the Tanjong Malim schools. The Malay teachers' school is extremely well equipped; about a hundred men are there at one time, doing a three-year course. Their work is all in the vernacular, but they learn to use two scripts—their own and ours. It is no doubt good to encourage them to see the world as Malays rather than as denationalized English; and I could warmly approve their geography syllabus, which begins with Malaya, and then extends to the East Indies,

India, and China. But I think it is going rather too far to exclude English from the curriculum altogether. I did not see them at their normal work. A terminal examination was going on. They were writing on the blackboard. It was quite awe-inspiring to see the immense care with which each youth wrote every letter of our script, rubbing out half a word to remodel a single letter. Did any Westerner ever so whole-heartedly respect his alphabet as a work of art? I fear these Malayan teachers, if they saw the hideous scrawls on many blackboards in England, would suffer the same internal pangs that a true artist must feel when he sees the slapdash drawing of an inept sketcher.

Handicrafts are encouraged. I saw some of the men doing beautiful basket-work. Their teacher encourages them with new designs. Others who were not occupied with examinations were having religious instruction. Practically all Malays are Muhammadans; and there are clauses in the treaties with the Sultans which may be interpreted as precluding Christian missions among Malays—or at least as precluding any Government support of mission institutions. Nearly all the mission work is among Chinese and Tamils.

The little mission school at Tanjong Malim is remarkable. An Indian who had belonged to the Methodists turned Fundamentalist, and tried to "convert" the children in the Methodist school. So he lost his job, and started a little school of his own with support from the Plymouth Brethren. The school is now three years old. It has four or five classes, with about a hundred children, including a few girls; they comprise all the races; all the teaching is in English. Most of the children are Muslim or Hindu; I suppose some may be Buddhist. They all receive Bible teaching, and learn to sing evangelical hymns; and the head master assured me that they sing these hymns in their homes, their parents not objecting. It all seems very astonishing, and I cannot think what the final outcome will be. It looks like another case of simplicity achieving what worldly wisdom cannot do. But, after all, is the achievement really to be desired? I got some amusement from their exercise-books. "Few and short were the prayers they said" hardly seemed the right sentence for the children of such a school to be writing in their copy-books; and I trust that none of the poor little Malayan boys, when married, will need to know the answer to the question, If 13 hats cost so much, how much will 376 hats cost?

The following day E. M. took me by car to the fifteenth mile up a hill road that is being made through glorious jungle; he has to go once or twice a week to see that the health of the workers is being properly attended to. Without proper precautions a workers' camp in the jungle might speedily be decimated by malaria.

Short visits to Ipoh, Taiping, and Telok Anson followed. I need not record them in detail. At Taiping, a beautiful town just under the hills, a certain white epiphytic orchid is common. It bursts into flower about once a month. Most kindly it chose the day I was there; so the trees seemed to be garlanded with white streamers.

At Telok Anson I stayed with the D.s on the bank of the Perak river, with jungle and rubber-trees all around. The view from the bungalow carried me in mind to Miss Turner's island at Hickling Broad; and it seemed *quite* right to hear a common sandpiper's joyful trill from along the river bank. The tuft-headed woodpeckers and hornbills and grackles were an alien element. So was the row of gorgeous cannas. And the boats. Some, it is true, were rather like wherries on the Broads; but all the boats are shaped like ducks—a long neck for the prow and two narrow pointed wings at the back—and the small boats float very buoyantly on the water, being broad and flat aft. The local crocodile refused to show himself.

We visited a little Hindu temple, where were three photographs of a Hindu saint at Kuala Lumpur—not attractive to look at, but apparently he is a simple soul with psychic gifts. One of the Telok Anson coolies went to see him to get cured of an illness. The saint looked at him and said: "You have got this illness because you kicked your mother." The man had indeed kicked his mother. Very likely his own guilty conscience connected the two things, and the saint may have read his mind and accepted the connection. Anyhow, D. seemed to think that those who visited the saint often got a moral stimulus; and I think a good many get cured of disease, perhaps by suggestion. The *yogi* takes no fees.

Then, after a pleasant fifteen hours' sea journey', I had two and a half days in Penang, where I met l some very pleasant and intelligent Government servants. Perhaps it was significant that I not only got real political information from these Government men, but also was released from the eternal tin and rubber politics of Malaya and sweeping generalizations about the "natives", to discuss such things as modern English poetry, the comparative merits of Chinese and Indian art, and German statesmen of the early nineteenth century.

I had a glorious morning's walk through the jungle on Penang hill. At one point I heard a loud squawk from a big tree, and there beheld a splendid black woodpecker, with red tufted head. Black rollers, with azure in their wings and bright red beaks, flew and tumbled as they chased one another round the tree-tops near the summit of the hill. In Penang I found my old Chinese friend of Cambridge days, C. E. Lim. He is now a flourishing barrister. He took me to lunch, where I met his wife. She told me that some Chinese wives like to have husbands who smoke opium, as they can smoke at home, and it keeps them from worse vices. Her husband wondered if this was intended for a hint! To a traveller like myself, seeing from day to day the home life of Chinese and Indian, of British and Dutch, it is very easy to see that human nature is the same everywhere; but to the white man who settles in the Tropics the little home things that he misses and the little alien things that irritate day by day come to loom so large that he can only see the differences.

Malaya is a country where economic imperialism can be seen in its simplest form—naked and unashamed. I do not wish by saying that to prejudge the issue. The defence of economic imperialism appears to me to be this: the world's population is ever increasing; the Tropics are full of untapped wealth; the world needs to utilize that wealth; the white man knows how to develop that wealth to the best advantage; therefore he thinks it right that he should direct its development. And to the individual planter or other white business man the position presents itself thus: accepting what I have written as axiomatic, he comes out to the Tropics, takes upon himself "the white man's burden", lives a life that is unnatural and in some ways uncomfortable, and longs for the time when he can retire and live at home in England. Either he goes to the bad through drink and other vice, or he makes money as quickly as he can to get home soon. Government officials, of course, have fixed salaries, and so, I suppose, have most of the planters, so they cannot do much of this. And they sometimes complain of the fact. Pity the poor white man!

Then look at the other side. It is an unnatural existence for any white man. He cannot settle permanently in the country and bring up a family there. He must have servants to do everything for him; and if he is an Englishman he almost inevitably acquires that disgusting "superiority complex", which is the hallmark of almost every Englishman outside his native land—the quality which our Continental neighbours less politely describe as "hypocrisy". We judge others, but never see the beam in our own eye. The Englishman always speaks as if the races he rules suffer from inferiority complexes. It rarely seems to occur to him that he is responsible. And there is the appalling effect on his temper. I have noticed this in myself. My leave-taking from Malaya is rather sad to record, but I think I will do it. I had spent the evening with the B.s very pleasantly, and came on board by the 11 p.m. launch. My luggage had been brought from the hotel, and I found the man (an Indian) on board, waiting to be paid. I had changed all my money into Indian rupees except a dollar and a half and a little more. I thought a dollar (2s. 4d.) would be quite enough. I offered him that. He demanded two, and I immediately became annoyed with him. However, I paid him all the rest of the Straits money I had, and told him I could give him no more. He was dissatisfied, and insisted that he was losing if I did not pay him two dollars. As I became more angry he became more quiet and dignified. His colleague appeared, and instead of joining in the argument reasoned quietly with him and took him away. Of course, as soon as he had gone I was ashamed of my behaviour. So I followed him to the launch, and asked him (as I should have done at first) to explain just what he had had to pay to various coolies, etc. This he did, clearly and quietly, and it came to one dollar ninety; so I gave him an Indian rupee, and we parted in peace. All the honours of temper, dignity, reasonableness, and truthfulness were on his side. The ordinary white man, reading this incident, would probably say that he fooled me in the end. In fact, I know he did not; it was I who nearly cheated him (Malaya is a *very* expensive country). I suppose with another few months in the Tropics I should lose that sensitiveness to truth that saved me at the last moment.

I fear life in the Tropics does some harm to almost all white men and women. I do not just mean that it is hardly possible to be a strict teetotaller, unless you want to cut yourself off from ordinary society. I respect those who feel it better to give way here and there in what they reckon little things in the desire to be all things to all men, to show friendship and comradeship; but if only they could really achieve the "all men" instead of only "all white men"! Nor am I thinking of betting on horse-racing, though that appears to be a great curse in Malaya. Nor even of sexual misconduct. What I mean is that I see in nearly all I meet, especially those one meets casually on trains and boats, a loss of refinement, of true gentleness, of that consideration and courtesy and self-restraint on which we English pride ourselves. The Englishman in the Tropics often ceases to be a gentleman.

The problem is not mainly political. British administration is very generally respected. In the eyes of many business men in the East the administrators are *too* generous to the "natives". An American missionary in the school at Ipoh said that, after seeing the administration of the Dutch in Java and the Americans in the Philippines, he had the greatest respect for the British. Chinese and Indians have spoken to me of their respect for many of our administrators. In so far as there is a political problem the extension of the League Mandates system may help to solve it. A mandate for the Straits Chinese to govern Malaya, if properly supervised, might prove satisfactory. I wish I could be as confident that the League can help to solve the much more dangerous economic problems. But fundamentally all these problems of race contact are moral; and to human sight the moral problem looks insoluble. Indeed, I see no solution until we honestly believe that Christian principles are meant to live by: we must learn "to love and bear".

IX

Back in India,
March

I was astonished at the number of little islands we passed as we came up the coast of Siam and Lower Burma (or rather Tenasserim). I think they form the Mergui Archipelago. They are not fully charted, and most are uninhabited. I believe before the war the German Government was negotiating with Siam for a coaling station there.

When we reached Rangoon there was some excitement because a German cruiser was lying in the middle of the river. It had been there several days, and crowds of people went by launch to see it each day. Apparently the cruiser was taking young officers of the German Navy for a world tour, and it is said to be the first naval visit paid by a German boat to British ports since the war. We are getting on! I had to confess to myself that I had more friendly emotions towards it than if it had been a French cruiser. It left its moorings at the very moment when we were starting down the river. The sound of its band playing, and the sight of all those fine young men on board, quite went to my head. We had a French lady on board. She seemed to have no ill feeling towards the boat or its occupants, but was quite determined that war must come never again—"jamais, jamais". I wonder now whether they have been secretly negotiating for one of those Siamese islands as a first step towards the rebirth of the German Empire!

Our boat stayed three days in Rangoon before continuing to Calcutta, and I found it easier to stay on it than to transfer to the Calcutta mail boat. This gave me a little time to learn something of Burmese problems. C. F. Andrews had put me in touch with an Indian member of the Provincial Legislative Council and of the Nationalist Party. He has taken up the opium question, and written articles attacking the Burmese Government. I also had a letter of introduction to Sir William Keith, Finance Minister. I went to Mr. T.'s office, and found he was at the Council Chamber, so after telephoning I went there, and after a little talk he took me up to the visitors' gallery where he sat with me and explained things. There was only one other occupant, an Indian lady journalist. But I think there was another gallery with three or four other people. All the Indian legislative bodies are discussing finance at this time of year—that is to say, in the National Assembly at Delhi and in all the Provincial Councils a grand assault is being made upon the Government, first for levying what are regarded as iniquitous and excessive taxes, and secondly for wasting them all on the army, the police, highly paid British officials, and dozens of other unnecessary trifles, instead of developing education, agriculture, and other "essential public services".

The Burmese Council provided a very fair sample. (I hope that everyone knows that Burma—though inhabited predominantly by a Mongolian, not an Indian, people—is one of the provinces of British India. Whether it should be is a hotly debated question. It is a country that is not at all fully developed; the rice cultivation is being increased greatly year by year, chiefly by imported South Indian labour. Rice is exported. The Burmese and the Indians naturally have different views as to which party gains or loses by this. The Burmese are inclined to think their country is being colonized and exploited to suit India, and that they have to share the weight of India's poverty and debt; the Indians think the Burmese ought to be grateful for having energetic immigrants who are adding to the wealth of their country. However, all this is by the way. I should add, though, that Burma is not connected to India by railway or road: near the coast there are too many broad rivers to bridge; farther up there are too many mountains, except right in the north, where a railway could be brought through hundreds of miles of unadministered Upper Burma across to Assam—but, except during the monsoon season, no one would want to go all that way round to Calcutta instead of the present two- to three-day sea passage from Rangoon.) This digression may be considered as equivalent to the first speech, which was in Burmese, so that neither the British members of the Council nor I could understand it. Is it not really amazing that men should be appointed as Ministers to defend their policy in a Council when they cannot understand the language of the country! I suppose they must all learn French and Latin, and perhaps Greek, before they can pass into the Indian Civil Service, but the language of the country to which they are going does not seem to matter. In fact, I believe they must pass an exam. in one or two "vernaculars", but it is a rather elementary exam., and many learn no more, but depend on interpreters. It may be said in reply that there are so many languages in India. But, in fact, Hindi (or Hindustani), Bengali, and Tamil (or Telugu) will cover a great part of India, with Marathi and Gujarati as the next most important; and Burmese for Burma. Apparently even at Calcutta a speech in Bengali was not followed by the English Ministers, or at any rate by some of them. Of course, it was very comforting for me that most speeches were in English, but that hardly justifies the position!

The next speaker in the Rangoon Council, one of the Burmese Nationalist leaders, spoke in English. I found the whole atmosphere very unpleasant. The speaker was obviously struggling to express himself in a language that he had not really mastered, and to make effective criticism of men whose mentality he did not understand (nor they his); he made rather wild generalizations and allegations, but the Ministers, instead of listening to him patiently, and allowing him to try to show what he was really driving at, insisted on interrupting time after time, so that he never got well into his speech and his time was up. The President (an Englishman) did not even give him a warning bell—this was, at the least, a breach of custom and courtesy. I met him at lunch the next day, and he said the President had apologized to him, but he intended to make his next speech in Burmese, so that he would not be interrupted!

I visited Mr. T.'s home the same evening, and met some of his fellow members of the Council—Indian and Burmese—next day at lunch. One of these, who had formerly been a Government official, but was now a Swarajist, really talked in a way that I could follow. I suppose he had more experience of Western mentality. He said that it was very difficult to get the Government to accept any proposal put forward by the popular representatives. He was one of those who liked to have a decent relationship between Government and Opposition; but he found the Government quite impervious to suggestions, even on minor matters concerning local incidents and interests.

There are, of course, some officials who are of Burmese race, including one or two Ministers. I had some talk with the Assistant Secretary for Education, a young Burmese aristocrat. He was concerned that primary education is too literary.

It is interesting to note that practically all the main objections raised to Indian self-government are inapplicable in Burma. There is no communal strife, no awkward native States, no caste system or depressed classes, no serious problem of frontier defence; and there is a very widespread system of primary education. Does the British Government, therefore, allow fuller responsibility to the Burmese than to other Indian provinces? On the contrary, the application to Burma of the 1919 reforms was delayed several years.

As you come up the Rangoon river from the sea you see beautiful pagodas in the villages; most of these taper to a narrow, tall "spire", which is usually brilliantly gilt. But the most famous of all these pagodas is in Rangoon itself—a glorious spire rising higher than the top of St. Paul's Cathedral, and surrounded by scores, if not hundreds, of Buddhist temples, many of them very beautiful, and some the gift of quite recent benefactors. The pagoda and temples are reached by a long flight of steps, with bazaars on each side. At the bottom of the steps all visitors must take off their footgear and walk barefoot. It seems that Europeans were allowed to go shod until ten or fifteen years ago, and the Europeans of Rangoon now refuse to go there, as they think the enforcement of the rule is a "political manœuvre". The fact that my fellow countrymen behave like silly babies did not seem to me to be a sufficient reason for doing the same. So, breaking the Englishman's vow, I went and saw the place. I noticed that my guide assumed that I was an American, though he seemed puzzled at my lack of explosive ecstasy.

The open pavements round the central pagoda were very hot to walk upon, and some places were very gritty; but you can bathe your feet under a tap before you put your shoes on again.

Now, of course I ought to try and explain what it is all like; but I am no good at that sort of thing, so I will not try. After admiring all the temples, and the costly presents that devout and wealthy Buddhists had presented, I was finally conducted by the guide to a place where various worshippers were kneeling at their prayers (if Buddhists do pray—I do not know) before some candles. He took me past these to where a priest was standing, and I found I was expected to kneel down, and the priest put his finger on a gilt image and then pressed the gilt on to my hand (or my brow—I forget which). Then, as I expected, he demanded rupees. Being extremely short of money, I refused to give him more than one rupee, and I thought I had got off fairly cheaply. He evidently thought me a poor sort of American millionaire.

There are a number of Chinese in Rangoon, but they are extremely particular not to allow any of their fellow countrymen to come into the country as coolies, or for any kind of lowly manual labour. They are all merchants and business men. Thus, nearly all the Rangoon coolies, including all the rickshaw men, are Indians. I saw no sign of elephants at work, though I believe there is one teak-yard across the river where they are still used, as a curiosity for visitors to see. The heavy work that ought to be done by elephants is done by unfortunate Indians. Along the docks every day, all day long, one could see fearfully heavy two-wheel carts being propelled by these "beasts of burden", two in front and two behind. If a wheel got into a rut it was ghastly to see the efforts of the men to get it out again. It is bad enough to see horses pulling at such loads. Was it foolish sentimentality, I wonder, that made me, in spite of these horrors, feel more comfortable and peaceful to be back in a dirty, dust-blown, noisy, casual Indian city, with the kites soaring overhead and no sense of the urgent march of civilization, after the prim tidiness of Java and the luxurious efficiency of rubber-tyred Malaya? In spite of poverty and exploitation, one felt that here again humanity could sprawl about in the streets for hours and forget.

Well, it is time to move on to Calcutta. For this second part of the voyage the boat was packed full, as a lot of small boys were returning to the Catholic school, St. Joseph's, at Darjeeling, for their nine months' term, after the three months' Christmas holidays. I shared a cabin with an American missionary and an Indian business man, who was relieved to find that his fellow passengers were human beings. He tried to persuade me that all the present religions of the world would give way to a new world religion. I told him I thought different peoples found help through different religious forms and ideas, but that I saw no reason why they should strive against one another, but this did not satisfy him.

He told me that a very amiable, grey-haired Indian on board was a great employer, Mr. Morarjee, with big cotton mills and shipping interests, and that he was going to Geneva to the Labour Conference in June as the Indian Employers' representative. I had some talk with him, and he told me how difficult it is for Indian shipping companies to compete with the P. & O. and B. I., as they take all the Government mails, etc. Lord Inchcape had said to him, "We have had the monopoly for seventy years—why should not we go on having it?" He quoted the whole of that "purple passage" in Macaulay's *Essay on Warren Hastings*, where he replies to the criticism that Burke had never been to India; showing how Burke had made every scene of Indian life live in his imagination. Mr. Morarjee seemed to find the second-class passengers more congenial than the first-class, and he helped to organize sports for the small boys one afternoon.

Soon after we left Rangoon I was the witness of a disgusting example of rampant imperialism—one of the first-class passengers shouting at one of the stewards, and ordering him to do absurd things, which he could not do and could not understand, and so reducing him to a state of bewilderment and misery, apparently with no other motive than sheer cruelty. I marvel at the way Indians respond to this kind of treatment. To describe their attitude as cringing is, I think, a gross libel. Rather, it is that patient meekness which is supposed to be one aim of Christian character. Several times when I have seen Indians brutally bullied like this the look in their faces has reminded me of the words, "Father, forgive them, for they know not what they do". Perhaps this will explain why I have come to doubt whether England has any mission to the East.

As we came up the Hooghly to Calcutta on Sunday morning, February 26th, I was delighted to see some trees with real fresh green foliage; and the public gardens in Calcutta were a blaze of colour. It was very odd to see beds of dahlias, pansies, snapdragons, phloxes, and other things all in flower at once. The yellow pansies really did send one's imagination away to the opening primroses and violets of the English hedgerow, and I felt terribly homesick because I knew I was missing the wonderful time when winter and spring struggle together.

Within a few days Calcutta was suffering from a fierce spell of early heat, and the pitiless sun seemed likely to shrivel up everything that was green and bright. And how can you talk of spring when all the grass is brown and dry?

Nalin Ganguly met me at the wharf, and took me again to the Y.M.C.A. I met some more of the typical young English business men there, and I made an interesting discovery about them. It really applied also to those I had met before. The recognized opening for a conversation with a stranger about India is to abuse all Indians as incompetent, untrustworthy, deceitful, and so on. You laugh and remain silent—at least I do; it is no use trying to refute them, for of course *they* know and you do not. But you wait. In a short time they will begin to tell you what a good fellow their servant is (though most Indians would tell you that an Englishman's servant is usually the most worthless type of Indian), and how some Indian in their business once did something very remarkable, and so on. In fact, like most people, these men are better than their creed. Only, unfortunately, the creed has to be reckoned with.

During my few days in Calcutta Nalin Ganguly and his brother Alin showed me much kindness. They live in true Indian simplicity; Nalin's room is reached by a steep outer staircase, which is almost a ladder. I told him that it suggested to me the steep ascent to Heaven. I found that some of his Y.M.C.A. colleagues object to his cheap Indian clothing, and tell him they hardly like to invite him to meet their friends. This is the sort of thing that almost drives one to despair. I suppose Christ, with his rough hands and common clothes, would never have been allowed in their drawing-rooms, though no doubt they have sentimental misrepresentations of him all over their walls. However, I suppose one must try to be gentle even towards those who seem to be unchristian Christians. I spent an afternoon and an evening at the Gangulys' house. On the latter occasion Nalin invited three of his friends, and we had a very interesting talk, chiefly about India's economic disabilities. One of his friends, Chatterjee, was a Cambridge economist, so I knew he would not mislead me! He asked me to tea at his house a few days later. Nalin also came, and he invited an old King's contemporary of mine, B. M. Sen. Also Chatterjee's elder brother and his wife were there. The elder brother is a great student of art, and he showed me magnificent illustrations of the Ajanta Cave paintings and other Indian art. I could hardly have had a happier initiation into the meaning of Indian art, and I came away with the feeling that I might, with prolonged study, be able to appreciate it. Some of the figures are very beautiful. It is easy to see that there is a rare sense of design and of form in much of this ancient art, and in modern Indian art too. But their attitude to nature is very different from ours. Buddha seems to be as central in ancient Indian art as Christ is in Western medieval.

Nalin also took me to call on Professor Radhakrishnan, and we there met other learned men. Professor Radhakrishnan had some amusing tales of people he had met in England. The Labour Clubs at Oxford and elsewhere had all declared that England could not possibly allow India to control her own tariff policy, as that might destroy the livelihood of the workpeople in Lancashire. The only leading statesman he met who seemed to appreciate the Indian point of view was Haldane, who said we English were too hopelessly unimaginative to be able to understand the needs of India or the real reason for her discontent.

One of the things we discussed at the Gangulys' was the economic impoverishment of Bengal, and especially the silting up of its waterways. During the following days I heard and saw a good deal more of this. For I went to see Sister G., who is a nun in the Anglo-Catholic Oxford Mission of the Epiphany at Barisal. This means five hours in a rather slow train, and nearly twelve on a river boat each way. I suppose Barisal is 150 or more miles east of Calcutta, across the Ganges delta. One of the chief troubles on these Bengal waterways is the dreadful water hyacinth, which since its introduction from America has completely blocked some rivers and canals. Also, of course, the rivers tend to change their course from year to year, so some streams gradually silt up and stagnate, bringing loss and poverty and malaria to the villages on their banks. Government cannot keep them all dredged. It dredges those that connect important places. It is a very difficult problem, but I cannot see on my present knowledge that the Government has much responsibility—unless it is true that far more silt is brought down from the Himalayas since the rather indiscriminate destruction of the forests just below them.

When I returned from Barisal I spent a couple of hours one afternoon listening to the debate in the Bengal Provincial Council. The room is long and narrow, and as the visitors sit at the two ends it is almost impossible to hear anything. The grounds of attack on the Government included the silting up of channels and increase of malaria in Lower Bengal. The attendance was so small that the Government did not choose to reply, and the debate was consequently adjourned.

Since I left Calcutta, Sir William Willcocks, of Sudan fame, has been lecturing there on the possibility of better irrigation in Bengal; and he says that if a seven-mile dam were built across the Ganges in Upper Bengal a magnificent flood could be brought down all the existing channels, and many more, to the enormous advantage of the whole country, both for destroying malaria and for increasing cultivation. I hope the Government will be able to set this in motion soon, by way of atonement for some of the evils Bengal has suffered in the past 150 years.

Barisal is in the Muslim part of Bengal. Sister G. said there are more Muhammadans in East Bengal than in (I think it is) Persia, Arabia, and Egypt all put together. They are, as generally in India, ignorant and backward; and there are far more crimes of violence among them than among the Hindus. But, as Father Strong said, the people of India all have a wonderful religious sense. He added that they have little moral sense, and they have not learned the connection between the two; but their sense of God is, none the less, a genuine thing, not mere superstition; and it therefore provides a most fruitful soil for the cultivation of good living. Sister G. spoke of *Mother India* as a wicked book. I have yet to meet a lady missionary in India who speaks well of it. At Barisal they live very simply, wearing sandals and no socks or stockings. I was housed for the day in a little thatched hut with a mud floor; and this was in keeping with most of the accommodation. There are schools for boys and girls, who learn agriculture and handicrafts as well as book-learning. For a time they spun *khaddar* each day, but they could not make it pay—carpentry pays much better.

I had proposed going to Santiniketan for the weekend to report to C. F. Andrews on my journey, and to discuss opium and other problems with him. On Friday, to my great joy, he appeared in my room in Calcutta, and proposed that we should travel together the following morning; and this we did.

When we reached Santiniketan I found that the following Tuesday was their spring festival, so I arranged to stay for it. It was delightful to be there again and to meet old friends, as they seemed to be. On the morning of the spring festival Rabindranath Tagore read several new poems in Bengali, written for the occasion, one by J. J. Vakil. He has written poetry with success in Gujarati (his own tongue), Bengali, and English. I did not see much of the poet this time. I had tea with him one day and tried to encourage him about his proposed visit to England. Lord Sinha had been telling him that since the publication of

Mother India people in England are very cold towards Indians. I assured him I believed there were many people in England who were perplexed and bewildered by that book, and who wanted reassuring; and C. F. Andrews agreed that Tagore is himself the best possible living answer. Before I left he gave me his blessing.

Famine now faces the country round Santiniketan; the ground is getting dreadfully parched; how the poor cattle can keep skin and bones together, as they move in herds across the land, grazing optimistically where there appears to be nothing to graze upon, is a mystery. And there are yet three months before the rains. Some of the wells are nearly running dry. While I was there a deputation came from a village to tell C. F. Andrews of their water shortage and to plead for his help. It struck me as significant that they came to him—the man in whom all trust, the friend of the poor—rather than to the local official. I have nothing against the local official; I know nothing for or against him. Very likely he is a good fellow who would do all in his power; but the people's faith is in Andrews. Santiniketan has appointed a committee, with Vakil as secretary, to organize special relief. They are sinking a big new well for irrigating some of the parched land, and raising relief funds in Calcutta. Government famine relief is apt to leave the people so very near the starvation level that this local help will be immensely valuable.

At Sriniketan (the agricultural school and experimental farm) I found things terribly dried up, and some little calves nothing but skin and bones; but at least the Rhode Island Reds and the silk-worms were fat and flourishing.

On the great day, the day of the spring full-moon, after several days of fierce heat, a strong north wind sprang up; all day the sky was full of dust, so that the sun was pale and washy, nor was the moon shining in full glory at night. Early in the morning the community gathered among the mango trees, where a place had been prepared with all sorts of strange and charming decorations, and girls and boys, maidens and men, came singing songs of springtime. After the songs the poet read poems written for the occasion. But I did not much enjoy that morning ceremony. I was too conscious of the absence of real spring, or what I call spring: my thoughts were in England; and probably I wanted my breakfast.

The evening performance, on the other hand, was unlike anything I have ever seen. It revealed to me the poet's greatness in a way that I had not understood before. It is a drama of springtime, which has been translated into English, so some readers will know it. Alternate choirs of youths and maidens come on the stage singing and dancing with the joy of springtime; the youths try to infect Dada, the serious student, the "cargo-boat of moral maxims", at first without much success, but to their own and the audience's amusement. The maidens are concerned with another frosted character, namely, Winter himself; and their efforts finally succeed in transforming Winter into Spring. Meanwhile the youths have resolved to try to bring Death himself, and infect him with springtime joy. They set out to find him, and plead in vain with the Ferryman and the Watchman, who think them quite mad. They find other sorrowful people on the road, and try to cheer them up, but everyone thinks them mad, and at last they become weary and disillusioned. Their Leader has disappeared, and they think he has led them astray. The little stream had seemed to say, "Forward, forward!" but what it really said was "False, false!" The world is all false. They had thought movement was heroic, but now they say: "Not to move, that is heroic, because it is defying the whole moving world."

They are saved from their clever disillusion by the laughter of one of their comrades, Chandra, who brings with him an old blind minstrel, who, he says, can lead them to the Old Man. The minstrel explains how he can find the way: "When the sun of my life set and I became blind, the dark night revealed all its lights, and from that day forward I have been no more afraid of the dark." "Those who have been made immortal by death", he says, "have sent their message in these fresh leaves of spring. It said: 'We never doubted the way. We never counted the cost: we rushed out: we blossomed. If we had sat down to debate then where would be the Spring?'" So they all rise up and follow the blind old minstrel, who sings as he walks. "1 cannot find my way", he says, "if I do not sing."

He leads them to the entrance of a dark cave; here, he tells them, their companion, Chandra, who has gone on ahead again, is seeking for the Old Man: he has left the message, "I will conquer and then come back again." But they wait and wait and he does not come; and they are ready to despair. They cannot live without their loved companion.

At last they notice that the blind minstrel has begun to sing a happy song of victory. Chandra comes, followed by the Leader himself. They learn that the Old Man, the enemy, he "who would like to drink up the sea of youth in his insatiable thirst", is a dream and a delusion. The enemy, Death, is no other than man's friend and ally, Life, in another guise. So the whole company, maidens and men, even the sober student, rejoice together.

The setting of the play was beautiful. A few trees were cleverly used, with the addition of bamboos stuck in the ground, to make a background for the stage. One or two coloured patterns had been drawn on the ground, and a few pots of flowers stood about. Electric lights had been ingeniously fixed in the trees and on the ground so as to shine on the dancers. It was remarkable how graceful and easy the dancing, was; it was almost more of a frolic than a formal dance; but although each youth or maiden seemed to be "frolicking" apart, yet they never got into each other's way; all was done in natural unison.

The poet himself took the part of the blind minstrel; his wonderful voice made what he spoke full of meaning, even to one who could not understand a word of it.

My words cannot possibly convey the power that brings conviction in the climax of the play. It was the truth of Easter, as seen by an Indian prophet—the unfathomable mystery of experience, that sorrow and death are transformed into joy and life. Some will say this Indian version is only an impersonal image; it lacks the human form on the Cross. Well, I did not feel that. It had, to me, the same real value that, I suppose, the mystery plays have had in Christendom. The blind old minstrel was the suffering hero, whose words compelled awe and wonder and devotion. Chandra was the heroic soul, conquering fear and pain with the spirit of joy. I will not press the parallel too far, but it seemed to me that the essence was the same.

The day after is the gala day for all young India, when every youth goes rushing about throwing bucketfuls of red water or handfuls of red dust over everyone. And for the next few days as you go about the country you see people in garments absurdly streaked and blotched with bright red. People with the fœtid imagination of a Miss Mayo would discover all sorts of beastliness in this ritual. I observed nothing but the most refreshing outburst of "animal spirits". Forewarned, I wore ancient clothes; but in fact I was let off with a red mark on my forehead—and that very easily came off again!

Lots of visitors from Calcutta and elsewhere came for the spring festival. At the play I found myself sitting between a young Calcutta business man, called Ganguly, and J. C. K.'s successor in the Chair of Economics at the Scottish Churches College, Professor Bhattacharyya; he remembered me from my visit to the College. So I was able to pursue my researches into the economic inequalities and grievances of India. Business-man Ganguly told me that the banks usually refuse credit to Indian businesses; but they will provide loans for any Tom, Dick, or Harry of an Englishman who wants to start or develop a business. Perhaps this is an exaggeration, but so long as the banks are British no doubt there is a strong tendency this way.

I travelled to the junction with Professor Bhattacharyya on the following day, and he gave me some of the reasons for the impoverishment of Bengal. One is that many of the natural leaders of the villages drift into the towns; and the *zemindars* spend their rent in Calcutta instead of fostering agriculture. So agriculture is carried on with less and less skill, and useful processes tend to be neglected and forgotten. Bengal and Bihar badly need a revision of the "permanent settlement" of 1789, which makes the lot of the *zemindar* much too easy. Owing to the change in the value of money the land is now worth nearly three times what it then was, although much has gone out of cultivation; the State gets nothing from this change—it all goes to the *zemindars,* many of whom no longer fulfil their proper function as "fathers" of the peasants. Indeed, the British have introduced a landlord system which is foreign to the Indian mind, and is still not understood by the peasants. This landlord class is a drain upon the land, and a major cause of its impoverishment. (I hope I have got this right; if I have not, it is my fault—I am no economist.)

My only stop on my way to Delhi was for a single day in Patna—from 5.30 a.m. to 10.30 p.m., a full, interesting day, spent mostly in the company of the Imam family. I was particularly glad to spend a day in a Muhammadan household. Hassan Imam, my host, is a wealthy lawyer, an elderly man, a Nationalist, who has always been inclined to put India before Islam. His brother, Sir Ali Imam, would pass anywhere for a high-class English gentleman. He has been a co-operator with Government until recently, but the appointment of the Commission has turned him into a whole-hearted boycotter. It is really fantastic that the Government should have ridden rough-shod over such sane, safe men. The anglicized Indian is still an Indian, and Lord Birkenhead, by treating them with contempt, has roused their spirit. "Is this", they say, "the reward of life-long unpopular devotion to an alien Government whose promises of development for self-government and declarations of equal status we have accepted at their face value? If so, know that the answer we give you is war." Hassan Imam has obviously found it painful to see some members of his family becoming Europeanized. At the same time he has sent his sons, too, to English public schools, to give them that self-reliance which in his view India lacks, and on which alone independent nationhood can be built. I could not help wondering whether it was safe to suppose that Indians at Harrow would acquire self-reliance without becoming anglicized in an evil sense. Neither of the brothers Imam sees the slightest prospect of England recognizing the justice of India's claims. Sir Ali Imam asked me what difference there was between the three English parties, and answered his own question to his own satisfaction by saying that there was none: all were equally based on national self-interest. Hassan Imam quoted Elphinstone ("the greatest man England ever sent to India") as having declared that it would be the proudest day in English history when England found herself bound to yield her rule to the people of India, and he took this to mean that sooner or later India would force England (not necessarily by bloodshed) to withdraw. But an independent India would be certain to destroy the economic prosperity of Britain; so Britain would never yield except to compulsion. This is the deadlock as most intelligent Indians see it, and they welcome the honesty of a Joynson-Hicks who admits it in preference to the hypocritical talk about "sacred trusts".

The Hindu editor of a Nationalist paper, a charming man, took me to see the Minister of Excise, an Indian. I hoped to say something to him about opium in Orissa, but he preferred to do the talking himself. He seemed an amiable old reactionary, but in any case I suspect that the Commissioner of Excise (an English official), largely controls policy: that seems to be the usual condition. But the Minister of Excise has gained respect by living on one-fifth of his official income and refusing the rest—quite a good precedent. This Hindu editor told me an interesting thing. He comes from the country, and during the war he was living in his village. He said the people were so confident and hopeful of the defeat of the British that he found it difficult to persuade them of British successes. When I mentioned this to a leading Indian in Patna he expanded it from his own knowledge of the villages. They applauded Boer successes in the Boer War, Japanese successes in the Russo-Japanese War, they deplored the defeat of Turkey in the Balkan War. In the Great War they even rejoiced over the fall of Kut, though Indian soldiers were defending it; and at the end of the war they wanted to know who these cursed Americans could be, who had come to rescue the defeated English. I may add that I have English authority for the belief that much of the "voluntary" recruitment, especially in northern India, was due to pressure.

Since I reached India again the Muslim Fast of Ramazan has been going on. In Calcutta one could see men with their praying-mats prostrating themselves out on the *maidan* day after day. Every good (or at least old-fashioned) Mussalman fasts from before sunrise to after sunset. We were seeing some Patna sights in one of Hassan Imam's motors about six o'clock when my companion (the Hindu editor) explained that the chauffeur wanted to stop to say his prayers at the mosque before breaking his day's fast. So we stopped and waited while he went up on to the roof of the mosque, and when all was duly finished he had a drink and ate a banana. I was hearing the other day of a class of Indians (Hindus and Muslims) here in Delhi who shouted with spontaneous laughter on hearing that a Christian "fast" consists in eating fish instead of meat. That is not what an Indian means by fasting. It is not surprising that Indians seem to be firmly convinced that every Englishman requires several courses of meat three times a day at least. The kind of meal that is served to a European on trains or in restaurants disgusts me nearly as much as it must an orthodox Hindu.

X

SATYAGRAHASHRAM, AHMEDABAD,
March 22, 1928

I reached Delhi on the evening of March 9th and left on the morning of the 21st. I stayed at St. Stephen's College, most of the time with Principal Mukarji and his wife. I found that he was a contemporary of mine at Cambridge. While I was in Delhi they had two College dinners—one of a college society, the other a farewell to two of the lecturers who are going to England for a year. At both these dinners Hindu, Muhammadan, and Christian students sat down together, and at both the students who served the food were also members of the several communities. At the former the Principal, in his speech at the end, suggested that the time might soon come when there should be only two messes in the whole college—the one vegetarian and the other meat-eating; and the students seemed responsive. At the second dinner about 150 sat down together.

The Mukarjis have been in England lately. When they arrived, Mrs. Mukarji told me, they were asked by everyone about *Mother India,* which they had not read. So she got a copy and began to read it; but it so infuriated her that she threw it down several times and I think never finished it. In Cambridge one lady almost refused to meet her; but she overcame the silly creature's prejudice by good humour. Generally she had found people in England very kind and considerate and without colour prejudice. It was her first visit.

Miss Campbell, President of the Women's Christian Temperance Union, who travels all about India working against drink and drugs, told me that her work has been terribly hampered by *Mother India.* She could not speak too strongly of the bad spirit animating the book and of its monstrous exaggerations. In Delhi I at last read Natarajan's reply, which is a series of articles republished from his paper, *The Indian Social Reformer.* It is a much more effective answer than I had been led to suppose. He shows that several of Miss Mayo's worst allegations are quite unfounded. For instance, the monstrous allegation that Hindu mothers commonly abuse their children is supported by not a shred of evidence, and is denied by, among others, Dr. Muthulakshmi Reddi, the woman vice-president of the Madras Legislative Council. The evidence against another unsupported allegation, of dedication of young boys to temple worship and their abuse by grown men, is quite conclusive. Similarly, the testimony of anonymous witnesses of very widespread venereal disease among educated Hindus is shown to be contrary to the actual evidence. And, of course, he easily shows that the Abbé Dubois's statements of 120 years ago, quoted by Miss Mayo as if they referred to quite modern times, are contradicted by contemporaries and by later witnesses, whose testimony is much more reliable. He makes short work of the fantastic first chapter. He shows that her use of the census reports is unfair. She entirely omits passages which show how rapidly the marriage age is rising; and he points out what any educated person ought to know—that child marriage is not an institution peculiar to Hinduism, having been the rule among Ancient Greeks and Romans, and among the English of the seventeenth century, none of them degenerate people. Again, she constantly assumes "that the marriage rite among Hindus means the same thing as it does among Europeans; whereas the fact is that in the Indian sense it is really a betrothal having the binding effect of marriage". He properly castigates her for her wicked misquotation and misrepresentation of Tagore's attitude towards marriage. I agree with the American he quotes, who says that the book reveals much more about Miss Mayo than about Mother India. He truly observed that "She is constantly involving herself and her readers in 'the fallacy of many questions', of which the stock example in the text-books is: 'Have you left off beating your mother, yes or no?' If the answer is 'Yes', it means that you were in the habit of thrashing your mother. If it is 'No', it means that you are still persisting in it."

I like, too, the way he uses her statement that "the only power that can hasten the pace of freedom is the power of the men of India facing and attacking the task that awaits them in their own bodies and souls." "That", says Natarajan, "is why most Indians feel that not till India's destiny is controlled by Indian hands—the British need not abdicate and go, but may remain and help—can there be any chance of a solid programme of reform being steadily put into effect, as has been done in Japan, and is being done in Turkey." "The British need not abdicate and go, but may remain and help." I am afraid a good many Englishmen in India would not accept such a position; but only those who are prepared for it can do much good in India to-day, I think. The more one hears the more disgusted one becomes with the whole *Mother India* affair. It seems to be a clever plot to incite all the worst possible race feeling.

One afternoon Miss Campbell, whom I have already mentioned, took me to an opium shop, the first I had visited in India for some months. One of the purchasers told us of a popular saying in Urdu which, when translated, signifies that opium "nourishes infants, ruins youth, and sustains old age". This does, in fact, represent the average ignorant opinion in many parts of India; and as long as it is believed Prohibition seems an impossible policy. But there are certain districts, especially Assam, where the evil wrought by opium is so manifest that no one believes in its efficacy at any age. In those districts Prohibition, enforced with reasonable regard to present addicts, would be generally welcomed.

Another curious incident happened at this opium shop. I was invited to sit down in the shop, while Miss Campbell asked questions of the people who came to purchase. As ever the vendor was most friendly and courteous, showing not the least resentment, though Miss Campbell told him frankly that she objected to the whole business. At the back of the shop was sitting an old man, who may or may not have been related to the vendor. I could not make out. He kept calling to me in Urdu, and Miss Campbell told me that he was pleading with me not on any account to begin taking opium. It did not matter about poor Indians; but it would be a dreadful thing for an Englishman to begin to take it. It was poisonous stuff and I should be ruined. I rather wished that certain officials I have met, who are quite sure that opium as taken in India does no harm and is accepted by every one as a good thing, could have heard the old man. I am afraid his fatalistic attitude about his own people is still typical.

For some days in Delhi I was rather unwell; so it was only at the end of a week that I was able to visit the Legislative Assembly and meet some of the leading politicians.

C. F. Andrews had given me a letter to Lala Lajpat Rai, asking him to introduce me to other members. I met him on Wednesday, and he arranged to get me an invitation to an "At Home" given by Srinivasa Iyengar (whom I had met in Madras) and Motilal Nehru to meet the President of the Assembly in the Assembly Courtyard on Saturday from 5.15 to 7. I then arranged to get a ticket for the Assembly gallery on Saturday, and so I listened to the debate all that day and went to the tea-party afterwards.

Before I describe the events of Saturday I think I had better try to explain the political situation, and the composition and powers of the Assembly, and the personalities of some of the leaders, as I expect some readers are not quite conversant with these things.

To begin with the composition of the Assembly. There are 102 elected members and 40 members nominated by the Government, of whom 26 are officials. This means that the officials have to act as parliamentary leaders and defend their policies in the Assembly: the leading members of the Civil Service are the official exponents of Government policy. Under these circumstances there is no Government party; but nearly all the nominated members and some of the elected members usually vote with the Government. The elected members include various representatives of "minorities"; Anglo-Indians are represented; commerce has its own elected representatives; the Sikhs and, much more important, the Muhammadans have separate representation. Some of the Muhammadans support the Government; others unite with the Opposition parties. The main Opposition parties to-day are: First, the Congress party, which is mostly Hindu, but aims at being a really national party, putting the interests of the nation above the interests of one community. Its leader is Pandit Motilal Nehru. Then there is the Responsivist party, led by Pandit Malaviya and Lala Lajpat Rai; they are more rigid Hindus, members of the Hindu Maha-Sabha, an important communal organization. At present they are inclined to try and outbid the Congress party in opposition to the Government. These two parties often act together. The Liberal party must also to-day be reckoned definitely as an Opposition group. It has only a few members; but they claim to be quite as ardently nationalist as the others—only they believe in different tactics. To-day, since the appointment of the Commission, they are much more vigorously in opposition than before. The Muslims are led by Mr. Jinnah, who tries to keep a united party, including on the one hand men like the Ali brothers, who are keen Congress members and who want to abolish the communal electorates in the interest of national unity, and, on the other, the Punjab Muslims, who regard themselves as Muhammadans first and Indians second, and who tend to support the Government.

In a full Assembly the Opposition can generally muster a majority, but it is never large. But there is no doubt, I think, that the Opposition parties together represent the vast majority of the electors. The electorate now includes over 5,000,000 men. In all provinces but one women are enfranchised, and are elected to the Provincial Councils; but they do not yet vote for the Central Legislature.

Incidentally I may mention that there is one member nominated to represent Indian Christians. Dr. Datta was at one time this member, and he took an independent line, and was, I think, generally respected. I think it would be better if there were no such nominated representative. Many Indian Christian leaders are opposed to any communal representation. The "representative" of the depressed classes (untouchables) is likewise a Government nominee.

Now, as to the powers of the Assembly. Many Indians would tell you impatiently that it has no power: that it is a mockery and a delusion. In fact, it seems to have real power over legislation: it recently rejected the Reserve Bank Bill by one vote, and that was the end of the Bill. But in finance its decisions are subject to the right of the Viceroy to "certify" things that have been rejected. Moreover, almost 50 per cent. of the Budget does not come before the House at all. Of late the Viceroy has been freely restoring what the Assembly has rejected. Under resolution of the National Congress held at Madras in December the Congress party is committed either to ignore the Central and Provincial Assemblies, or to attend them with the avowed purpose of opposing, and if possible defeating, the Government's financial measures. So it is hardly surprising that the Viceroy certifies what the Assembly rejects. And then the Swarajists can and do naturally retort that the whole thing is a farce.

Well, now I must explain what happened on the Saturday when I listened to the debate. When I arrived the proceedings were very dull; two Opposition back-benchers were moving a series of amendments to the Finance Bill, aiming at reducing the proportion of taxation payable by the heads of large Hindu families, who live all together in more or less patriarchal fashion. Sir Basil Blackett, Finance Member of the Government and leader of the House during the spring session, which is devoted to finance, replied, as I thought, effectively. He said most of the proposals put forward in the name of equality of taxation were really proposals to give preferential treatment to some particular class or community; and he tried to show (I think he did show) that in fact the heads of Hindu households suffer no injustice under the present arrangement. The first amendment was defeated without a division. Then the President, Mr. Patel, proposed that as the other amendments, all put down by two men, were really identical in purpose, they could be ignored. He had a little altercation with the two members and finally allowed them to speak to one other amendment; but he interrupted them once or twice and insisted that they should confine themselves strictly to the point of the amendment (why the reduction should be by 50 rupees rather than by 100, or whatever it was, which had already been defeated), and so he soon stopped them and a division was taken, resulting in a Government victory, and the other amendments were not allowed. Then Sir Basil Blackett formally proposed the final reading of the Finance Bill. I think he had expected nothing more than a formal division; but in fact the Opposition took the opportunity to make a general attack on the financial and economic policy of the Government. Pandit Malaviya spoke first. His speech occupied nearly an hour and a half. For the first half-hour I thought it very forcible; later he became dull, and he seemed afraid to sit down for fear he had forgotten something that he might have said. I understand that he generally speaks at great length. He is popularly said to begin with Adam and come down to the present day. But as far as I remember there was not much ancient history in this speech.

The early part of his speech was mainly concerned with the Government's military expenditure. It was not a pacifist speech, but it seemed to me to be an effective demonstration of the essential imperialism of Government policy. He drew attention to the numbers of British troops (as opposed to Indian) in the country. There are 70,000, of whom 27,000 avowedly exist for keeping "internal order". Why, he asked, if your professions of faith in Indian loyalty to the Empire are honest, should we be called on to support all these expensive white troops? Why not rely on Indian soldiers entirely? There is no question of efficiency, and the Indian soldiers have constantly shown themselves ready to perform any duty. Five years ago there were 6,000 British officers in the country. To-day there are 7,000. Why this increase? The speech was of a conciliatory and persuasive nature. The Pandit made some polite remarks about Sir Basil Blackett, who is shortly leaving India, and insisted, I think quite sincerely, that the attacks of the Opposition had nothing personal in them; they all recognized Sir Basil's high qualities and financial ability. But he insisted that it would be undignified and impossible to vote for a Government that consistently refused to accept any of the proposals of the national parties.

After lunch the Indian representative of the Bombay Chamber of Commerce read a speech supporting the Government for all its virtuous financial achievements. At one point, where he solemnly read a statement that "time does not allow me" to develop the argument further, the President gaily intervened with "There is plenty of time", to the amusement of the House and the temporary discomfiture of the speaker. Several times during the day Mr. Patel intervened in this rather informal manner, usually with the purpose of speeding up the business, but more than once by pleasant sallies that broke the sense of boredom.

Then a Muslim back-bencher made an attack on the Government for giving disproportionately few Government appointments to Muslims. He had seemingly endless statistics of officials in the post office, the revenue department, the railways, and in every conceivable department in province after province. Some of his statements provoked much laughter among his Hindu neighbours. When I mentioned this speech to a Muslim student who is a leading personality at St. Stephen's he commented that the disproportion is due to the lack of education among Muslims, and it was rapidly righting itself, now that they are improving their education. I do not think he was referring specially to the Muhammadan University at Aligarh, whose low standard is at present quite notorious.

Then came a speech from a non-official Englishman, who was horrified at the prospect of the defeat of the Finance Bill—a thing that happened in 1924, the first year that the Swarajists took part in the Assembly, but has not happened since—and appealed to the Nationalists to consider what they were doing.

This brought Pandit Motilal Nehru to his feet, and he made a speech full of fire and energy. He was wholly unrepentant, and had even found it painful to listen to Pandit Malaviya making such earnest attempts to appeal to the stubborn hearts of the Government members. He accused the Government in some detail of complete failure to improve the economic condition of the country, and of complete lack of understanding of its real needs. He thought the exploitation of India was necessary to English prosperity, so it was useless to believe in England's fair promises; India must win her own freedom. When he sat down Sir Basil Blackett rose to reply; but several other Opposition speakers rose, too. The President asked Mr. Ranga Iyer if he could make his speech short, and he said he could; but he went on for over twenty minutes, and when he finished the President adjourned the House. Mr. Ranga Iyer is a Swarajist member who has written a book (said to be feeble) called *Father India*, in answer to *Mother India*. The burden of his speech, which was certainly able, especially in repartee, was "No taxation without representation". In other words, a parliamentary system that does not give real control of the purse is a mockery. He spoke of the Bengal *détenus* (i.e. men detained in gaol or at home without trial); and he insisted on using the hackneyed expression that these men were "rotting in the gaols and swamps of Bengal"; one, he said, had been "rotting" since 1923. I confess that this was too much for me. I could not help joining in the smile that spread over all the English faces. It is very unfortunate that these passionate Indian nationalists have to use a language in which their highest eloquence may suddenly strike the English listener as merely ridiculous. As I sat listening to this indictment of Government policy from member after member, my mind suddenly leapt across the ocean and the centuries, and I heard the Puritan leaders of the Long Parliament making their "Grand Remonstrance" against Charles I. Charles undoubtedly believed, not only that he was divinely ordained to rule England, but that his rule was for England's good; and some of those parliamentary leaders were narrow-minded men, caring more perhaps for their class interests than for the welfare of the "depressed classes" of their day. But tyranny is tyranny, however well intended; and the call to liberty is a noble call, even when it is not wholly free from selfish motives. As we honour Pym and Hampden, India will honour Nehru and Lajpat Rai.

The debate was continued on Monday, but I could not get to it. An Indian journalist (a Nationalist) whom I met on Tuesday afternoon told me that I had missed the best speech Sir Basil Blackett ever made. As a rule, he said, he cannot resist making sharp retorts and debating scores; this time he did resist the impulse. I have since read a very full report in the *Times of India*. It is a very interesting speech. After dealing with some financial technicalities, he comes to the main burden of the attack. Briefly, his defence of the Government amounts to this: That they have done something to increase education (from $5^1/_4$ millions in 1913 to $7^3/_4$ millions in 1926), but he admits that is not much; that there were no co-operative banks in 1913, but in 1927 there were 127; savings bank deposits have increased fourfold in the same period, and there have been other similar increases; much has been done, by irrigation chiefly, to increase the prosperity of the Punjab, and he mentioned several other "big projects of irrigation that are now well on the road towards completion". His reference to Brayne's book, *Village uplift in India,* hardly strengthens his argument; for if Brayne's work is so excellent, it might be said, why has not the Government encouraged officials generally to undertake such work, instead of leaving it to the initiative of an official whose real work is of another kind, and then (I understand) failing to promote him, on the ground that he had neglected his real duty! And if this is the full Government case on the economic side I think it is a poor one. I suppose he could have mentioned roads and railways, but they are not unmixed blessings. I am glad he did not point with pride to the sum of 15 crores (= 150 millions of rupees) already, with more to follow, spent on the new Delhi—a really wicked waste of a poor country's money.

I believe the notion that magnificence makes a good impression on Indian people is quite false. A sensible man like Blackett probably knows that.

The part of his speech that I like best is his answer to Motilal Nehru's statement of the conflict of interest between England and India. He insists that the best interest of England, so far as India is concerned, must come from the prosperity of India; and that India's true prosperity means the development of India by the people of India. He developed this further at a dinner the same evening, where he spoke of the remarkable development of Indian capital and Indian-owned industry, including jute and, still more remarkable, steel. I have been trying to persuade my

Indian friends that the true interest of India and England is the same, at any rate ultimately; so I am glad to know that such a distinguished economist insists on the same truth.

But even more significant, it seems to me, is Sir Basil's frank admission that the present time is more critical, and feeling more strained, than at any other time in the past five years. He, at least, has no illusions as to the gravity of the crisis precipitated by the appointment of the Commission; and although he cheerfully suggested that "the darkest hour may be the hour before the dawn", he had nothing to say of any sign of the dawn approaching.

I cannot see that he referred at all to Pandit Malaviya's attack on the military system. The Bill was passed by 61 to 41. Some Nationalists were certainly absent in accordance with the Congress resolution, but Blackett's speech must have turned several votes. I hope my summary of this debate is fair to both sides.

All members of the Assembly had been invited to Saturday's tea-party, but only one English member of the Government appeared. Feeling is very strained. Yet I found the Indian members I spoke to most amiable and friendly. I do not believe an Indian could be really rude, and standoffish, even if he wanted to be. The only way they can possibly keep up the boycott of Sir John Simon and his colleagues is by keeping well away from them.

In a letter from Geneva I had heard something about "continual bombing of villages on the north-west frontier". Having heard nothing about it here, I asked Lala Lajpat Rai (as a Punjabi), and he said he did not think any such thing had been happening for a long time past; but he called a young journalist, who said that there had been bombing about 25 days before, as "punishment" for a raid. The journalist was inclined to defend it as the quickest and most effective way of striking terror into people who owe no allegiance to any settled government (though more or less friendly to Afghanistan), who live by raiding their peaceful neighbours in the plains. Lala Lajpat Rai, on the other hand, denounced it as barbarous. But he did not suggest an alternative. I think it is a very difficult issue for a pacifist. I suppose every attempt ought to be made (perhaps it is being made) to establish peaceful intercourse with the warlike tribes, and supply their needs in exchange for any hill produce (as in Shillong, where I saw the hill people bringing their supplies to market). Meanwhile, not having been able to visit the north-west frontier, I cannot dogmatize about the right and wrong methods of "policing" it. It cannot be expected that Indian leaders, oppressed with the knowledge that millions of their fellow subjects are half-starved, will pay much attention to this subject.

I also discussed with some of the leading nationalists the new Constitution they are drafting. In the eyes of political India this is far more important than the activities of the Assembly. Practically all Indian parties are co-operating, and they have achieved a remarkable measure of unity already. The Hindu Mahasabha and some of the Muslims are difficult to appease over the question of communal representation. The principle generally advocated is the abolition of all communal representation, but reservation of proportionate numbers of seats for minorities. In Bengal, one of the critical provinces, all parties agree to this; but in the Punjab and Sind there are still difficulties, and accordingly the Conference has adjourned for six weeks, hoping to meet again in greater unity at the end of that time. Proportional representation is also under discussion. By a considerable majority they have accepted the principle of adult suffrage—in spite of illiteracy. It was felt that no literacy test would be really satisfactory, especially as it would cause fresh communal trouble. They contemplate constituencies with over 100,000 electors. The Parliament would consist of 750 members, representing at the beginning the 200 million inhabitants of British India. Muhammad Ali, who comes from one of the Indian States, told me he had been urging the desirability of going gently in that matter at present. He believes that once their great support (the British Government) has been withdrawn they will soon have to come into the new National State. Meanwhile, just as the treaties between the States and the East India Company were transferred to the British Crown in 1858, so they might be automatically transferred to the new Indian Commonwealth.

I am glad to find that there are clauses asserting the right of every child to receive education, certain workers' rights, and also sex equality.

Srinivasa Iyengar is visiting Europe this year to study modern constitutions. He is the "Alexander Hamilton" of the Constitution.

Muhammad Ali, with whom I had a long talk one day, told me a good deal about the discussions, especially of the communal issue. He was also very keen to point out that there have been no communal disturbances in India for five months now. The December eclipse might easily have provoked outbreaks; and since our talk the fast of Ramazan has ended in the great Muslim feast—I believe without any serious disturbance.

I found Muhammad Ali a charming man. He almost monopolized the conversation for two and a half hours. In the midst of it sunset came, so he took a drink of water (I suppose his first since sunrise) and retired to the other side of the room to say his prayers. On returning he started off again with the gay remark: "Having fulfilled my duty to God, I can now go on with my duty, not to Caesar, whom I don't recognize, but to humanity—that is, to you." And he did so at length, but all the time holding his audience's closest attention. This remark about Caesar really did not mean the British Government. When I arrived I found him surrounded with open Korans and commentaries, and at least one copy of the Bible (open at the Book of Judges). He was expounding to two of his assistants on the paper he edits (called *Comrade)* the thesis that the Koran and the Bible alike advocate theocracy and condemn monarchy. By theocracy he means republicanism, a republicanism that refuses to have any king but God. He made good use of the story of Saul and Samuel, and some curious legends about Solomon and Rehoboam.

He assured me that Islam does not preach a war of armed might: the "holy war" is a war of spiritual conversion. He has no fear of the Hindu majority in India, because it is being steadily converted to Islam. Islam is strong, not where the Moguls conquered and ruled, but rather in the outlying territories, as in Bengal, where missionaries were unhampered by the false authority of monarchs and armies. All other religions denote the place or person of origin; Islam alone bases itself on a great religious principle, obedience to the will of God. At one time I thought in his enthusiasm he was going to claim me as a convert to the faith. I have never been treated as a potential convert before, I think. It is a strange experience. Even if he had given me an opportunity to hint doubts or to suggest defects in his argument or in his religious system, I do not think I should have wished to take it. His enthusiasm and sincerity were quite disarming—and also quite unconvincing!

It was after eight when I got away, and I think his friends who were waiting for a meal must have thought me a tiresome visitor. I felt inclined to say to them, "Please, it wasn't my fault!"

He was at Oxford—a contemporary, I think he said, of Sir John Simon. Many of the Nationalist leaders are Oxford men. Does this mean that we at Cambridge treat Indians more kindly; or does it mean that the Oxford passion for politics extends even to her Indian sons?

I must not omit the great Muslim prayer of the last Friday of Ramazan, which I witnessed from the open ground below the huge Jama Musjid mosque. C. R., one of the college staff, took me there. Thousands and thousands of people came from all the country round on this special day. The mosque itself was packed with people, right up on to its towers; and there were thousands on the streets and the open *maidan* below it. Many women were there from the villages, clad in all the colours of the rainbow and a good many other colours; whilst a fair number of higher class women, clad in white and strictly veiled, had driven out from the town for the occasion. Though many of the people had taken up their positions half an hour before the time for prayers began, many were still trekking about, with little children straggling along behind, until almost the time; and there was no clock to show them the time. Yet when the moment came all were arrayed in lines in perfect order, with no one to marshal them. Then all with one accord, as the sound of the first cries of "Allah, Allah" came from the mosque, took up the cry and made obeisance, going down on their faces to say their silent prayers. Three times the process was repeated; then all was over, the whole thing lasting less than ten minutes. The spontaneous unity of action was astonishing to behold. I can only liken it to the swift manceuvres of a great flight of birds. If Islam can supply such unity of action it may well have a great future in India—unless the way to co-operation is learned through other means.

In Delhi I found an Englishman who was keen on birds, and we spent a delightful afternoon together in a park where darters nest in the trees on an island in a small lake. They are very odd birds. Several were sitting in the palm-trees, sometimes holding their wings open, exactly as cormorants do. In fact, they suggest cormorants in everything except their ridiculously narrow necks and heads. I have never heard of any evolution theory that would seem to account satisfactorily for a race of cormorants suddenly growing thin necks and small heads.

We sat on the ground and watched one fishing in the water. It evidently caught the fish by impaling it on its lower mandible under water. Then it came to the surface and shook its neck violently (has this violent shaking led to a gradual process of attenuation?) in order to shake the fish loose; the final jerk throws the fish into the air, and the bird catches it and swallows it. Once it got such a large fish that it stuck in its gullet, and the bird had to go under water again two or three times and drink some water to help wash it down—there are disadvantages in being narrow-necked.

At the beginning of my journey from Delhi to Ahmedabad I had an interesting talk with an Indian police official from Jaipur State. He talked about corruption in the police and Government services generally. He thinks superior officials can do a good deal by drastic treatment of all cases brought to their notice; and he said Sir Malcolm Hailey, Governor of the Punjab, does this. The difficulty is to be sure that you are not punishing a falsely accused man.

Surely there cannot be many countries in the world where you can miss the express train, and overtake it eight hours later, with half an hour to spare, by taking a slow train by another route. But this happened to me. At Rewari Junction I found that, as my train had no dining-car on it, I had better get lunch. An official assured me there was plenty of time (in fact, there was about twelve minutes) and that he would let me know when the train was going. They regularly do this for the British traveller. The train was at the front of the platform; the refreshment-room at the back. So I could not see the train while I ate. The waiters were quicker than usual, and I had practically finished and was expecting my summons when suddenly a scared official looked in. "Are you on the Jaipur train?" "Yes", I said. "But it has gone." "Can't you bring it back?" (They do in India—at least for a white sahib.) No, it had quite gone. The station-master was summoned. All officialdom came. We all racked our brains for bright ideas. They would telephone to the next station to put my things out (my books, papers, and maps were strewn over the seat; even my binoculars were casually sitting in a corner of the compartment—it was a small two-berthed compartment). Then I could go on by the next train, after eight hours, and pick them up there. But I had carefully arranged *not* to go by the train that reached Ahmedabad at midnight; so I demurred. Was there really nothing else to do?

Suddenly a light dawned in the station-master's eyes. "Yes, quick! You have just time to catch this train. It is going round by the desert. It will reach Sambhar half an hour before the other." We rushed along the platform; I jumped with the guard into the van of the moving train, the waiter panting along beside us to get his due (he got it all right); and at the next station the guard transferred me to a first-class compartment. At first I shared this with a Rajput rajah who had no English, and when he got out I was left alone. So the hours passed. It was a good discipline—a true Indian discipline. I tried to thrust from my mind the thought of my luggage, my intimate possessions, my binoculars: those little fretful, anxious fears that are far harder to combat than great catastrophes. I had no book, no food, no water, no human company; only the hills and the plains and the wayside stations.

I did not get very hungry or thirsty. I have been learning in India that it is easy to banish hunger and thirst for quite a long time. On long bird-walks in England I have found that absorption in other things can keep hunger away. But it has been a new discovery that one can put it out of one's mind even without anything much to take its place. You just say to yourself: "I shan't have food for a long time. I shan't need it"; and you don't need it, you forget about it. It is, for a normally well-fed person, one of the simplest forms of suggestion. I expect it is easier in the Tropics than in cold climates; but it seems to work, even for thirst.

After hours and hours of silent vacuity at last I reached Sambhar. I got some dinner. The train came in. I found the guard; the Rewari station-master had telegraphed to him. He had locked my compartment; he opened it for me. Everything was there, shaken about a little and covered with dust; the binoculars lying in their corner. So I went on writing my letter home, as if nothing had happened. Throughout this journey I have been rather neglectful of my property in spite of warnings; and nothing has been stolen. But let me not boast.

This slow train brought me by the edge of the desert, where goats and camels are the only common animals. The camels feed on the foliage of trees at this time of year, whilst men were pruning the trees to feed the goats. In other places there was a good deal of wheat, some of it being harvested. I saw one small patch of white opium poppy in full flower—a beautiful sight. I did not really come through the opium district; I believe this one patch was in Jaipur State, where its growth is now illegal. This reminds me that I noticed a few opium poppy plants in flower in the garden of the income tax office in Delhi. In British India its growth is illegal, and I thought it would be a pleasant jest to "inform" the police against the collectors of income tax. But in fact I connived at this breach of the law.

XI

Mount Abu
March

Now at last I come to Mr. Gandhi. Not having paid proper attention to T.'s instructions, I managed with some difficulty to catch a train out from Ahmedabad to Sabarmati, only to find, when I got to Sabarmati station at the hottest time of the day, that there was no possibility of leaving my heavy luggage there, and that the only way to get it a full mile to the ashram was on the heads of porters, who were more willing to carry it than I was to see them staggering along. But such is India. I ought to have driven from Ahmedabad. Coming this way, we passed through the precincts of the prison. It seemed rather symbolical that Mr. Gandhi should live so near a prison—as if to emphasize the contrast between the old dispensation and the new: and to remind the new that it has not yet abolished the old.

I found friendly people to receive me, and I was put in charge of a young German and a young Dutchman, on the ground that they would understand my needs. They were, in fact, most kind and helpful.

I was put in the room reserved for distinguished guests. It was a stone-floored cell, devoid of furnishing save for two or three packing-cases in one corner and three small shelves in the wall. It was at the eastern corner of the building and had four low windows with iron bars, so it was fairly cool. It was on the ground floor of a good-sized building of two stories, with a courtyard in the middle. This building is shared between visitors (downstairs) and schoolboys; older students and residents live in other buildings. There is also a small reading-room upstairs, containing a few periodicals in English, Gujarati, and Hindi.

Another building contains the infants' school upstairs (which unfortunately I did not see at work) and the library below. The library depends almost entirely on donations. Its basis consists of the books Mr. Gandhi had in his professional days.

Across the road there is the office, the building with an open courtyard, where cotton is combed and ginned and spun and woven by members of the *ashram* who are experts and by visitors who are learning. Members also have their own spinning-wheels in their own rooms. Then, close above the river bank, looking across to the factory chimneys of Ahmedabad, is the building in which Mr. Gandhi and some of his family live, and where also, on the veranda at the other end, visitors have meals. Fortunately this is placed rather high above the river, so it just escaped damage in the great flood of last autumn. The "National University", two miles away, was out of session, but I met one of its teachers. He wears *khaddar*, but he does not accept *ahimsa* (non-violence or harmlessness) for international affairs.

The fixtures of the day are: Early hymn-singing and prayers at 4.15 a.m.; early breakfast (being milk, and for the ravenous Westerner toast) at 6.30; a solid meal, Indian style, with rice as its staple, at 10.30; another such meal at 5.30; evening hymns and prayers at 7. The 4.15 a.m. event sounds rather alarming; but a bell is rung with such violence that no one can fail to wake; and there is nothing to prevent you from going back to bed and to sleep again from 5 till dawn, if you happen to be a Western dormouse like me.

Having been supplied, on my arrival, with two fine mattresses and a chair (which I lost two days later, as it was required for Pandit Motilal Nehru to sit on when he came for two days' talk with Mr. Gandhi), I rested till 5.30. At the meal I met a young American—a quiet, thoughtful man, who is trying to live without property. Another visitor was an Indian Christian, from the Christa Seva Sangh at Poona; we had good talk together. Then I went for a little walk and watched the sand-martins going in and out of their holes in the river bank. A family of four pied kingfishers that had evidently just emerged from a larger hole in the bank were sitting in a row on a little mud-flat, squeaking shrilly to encourage their parents to hurry up with the supper. The parents were doing their best, hovering over the water, and plunging now and then with a splash, emerging again usually with a fish that was brought to the noisy, ravenous children. As I was coming back, watching some red-breasted flycatchers that were still lingering here, I came upon another visitor to the *ashram* sitting under the trees—a man from Ceylon who has helped to start some social reforms at Kandy. We returned together to the 7 p.m. prayers, just as the sun was setting. It was very peaceful sitting on the ground in the little "square" just above the river and listening to the occasional cries of the birds: the fluting calls of waders, the sharp cries of various kingfishers, and the harsh squawk of herons. Gradually one after the other the members of the *ashram* came and sat down on the ground. There must be nearly a hundred in all. One brought a cloth and a pillow, the latter propped against the wall facing us—luxuries that I am sure Mr. Gandhi dislikes, but his health now makes them necessary. Then an erect figure, spare but neither thinner nor shorter than most of his fellow countrymen, comes stepping quickly, and without ado he has seated himself with his legs crossed, like the others. He folds an upper garment about his shoulders, and, I think, immediately closes his eyes to join in the chanting, which begins almost at once. But as I closed my eyes, too, I do not know what he was doing. At the end the names of all the members are called over, and each in turn says how much spinning he has done during the day. The calling of names begins the very moment prayers are ended. There is no break—no suggestion that we are turning from the sacred to the secular. It seems evident that Mr. Gandhi believes that *laborare est orare*, or, at least, that the two things are very intimately connected. The whole life of the *ashram* is a life of ascetic discipline. I found it almost intolerable to have no menial task to perform for the community. My Dutch friend insisted on sweeping out my room each morning; and I only once succeeded in outwitting him and getting it done before he arrived.

To return to the first prayer time. I happened to notice that, while the names were being called out and the record of the week's events read, Mr. Gandhi enjoyed himself by stretching out his hand as if to catch one or two small infants who were running about near him; and when he did catch them they crowed with joy. I found it hard to feel that I was looking on one of the great souls who have shaken the world. He has not the "presence" of Tagore. Perhaps he could show it, but he prefers to keep his great soul veiled behind his marvellous humility. So what you see is a man full of simple human emotions: very quick to understand, with a genius for giving and inspiring trust. I did not notice the flashing or even the penetrating eye. His eyes have, indeed, a beautiful expression, and when he comes to the point of something he is saying he looks at you with a quick glance that is very direct; his eyes seem to say: "Just *that* is what I mean; I hope you see." His face has the look of one who has undergone much spiritual conflict; but in his expression there is the peace that comes to those who have overcome.

I did not speak to him that first evening. I did not even know that he had heard of my coming; but when I had gone to bed—at about 9 o'clock—and was just beginning to think I ought to have tried to fix up my mosquito-net, the manager came with one or two youths, and, finding I was not asleep, explained that Bapu (meaning Father, or rather Daddy: that and not Mahatma is what he is called at the *ashram)* had wanted me to have a proper bedstead, and had I a mosquito-net? So they got me a bedstead, and we fixed the net, and I slept in peace.

Mr. Desai, Mr. Gandhi's secretary, a very fine man, kindly arranged for me to have a talk with him at four the next afternoon. Needless to say I was impatient for the hour to come, and looked at my watch a good many times. But, having been in the East for some months, I thought it more polite to arrive five minutes late. When I appeared Mr. Desai looked into Mr. Gandhi's room, and then said to me: "Do you mind waiting for a few minutes? He is not quite ready for you." That did not surprise me. What are ten or fifteen minutes to those who dwell in eternity?

But when I did go in his first words told me that he was no son of the East in the matter of time. "I am sorry to have kept you waiting," he said, "but at two minutes to four I asked if you had come, and when I found that you had not, I thought I had better have my milk" (he is on a very strict and plain diet) "so as to save time and give us more time for a good talk." Two minutes to four, indeed! And to save time! But there was not a suggestion of impatience in his tone of voice; just a simple, friendly explanation of his seeming lack of punctuality and of immediate hospitality to the invited guest.

He was sitting on the ground and spinning, also, as he explained, as he liked to be fully occupied all the time: it would not interfere with his freedom to talk and to listen. I essayed to sit on the ground, too; but he preferred that I should sit on a bench. Once or twice while he talked he broke his thread, and explained what a delicate touch is needed for the expert spinner, and how poor an expert he himself still was.

I gave him messages from the Mukarjis, from Miss Campbell and from Muhammad Ali; and then we got on to business. I told him that I had been inquiring into the situation regarding drink and drugs, opium especially, and I mentioned a few of my experiences and impressions. Then I asked him what his policy was and what he meant by "Prohibition".

He wants immediate prohibition of the import and sale of foreign liquor. All over the country, he says, there is a strong anti-liquor sentiment, and hardly anyone defends the liquor habit. Foreign liquor is chiefly drunk by people who like to ape Europeans, and they are ashamed of it in the presence of their fellow countrymen. But opium is rather different. He thinks he was himself probably "soothed" with opium in babyhood; and certainly his father took it to "sustain" old age. So long as this kind of use is generally regarded as right opium must continue; but he would bring it under medical control instead of having opium shops; and every bit of revenue should be put into a fund for propaganda against opium and for improving medical facilities or other measures essential to its ultimate suppression apart from strict medical requirements.

Then I told him there was another matter, more personal to myself, that I wanted to speak about; but perhaps I had stayed long enough. His health is very precarious. His *masseuse*—an English lady—had already told me that he is a most difficult patient, because he will not obey the orders of doctors and nurses. However, he was insistent that I should stay a little longer, so I put my "concern" before him. Perhaps I ought to explain that during these last weeks I have suffered more and more from the sense that no Indian seems now to believe in the possibility that we British as a people can ever understand their needs or meet them with generous, humble sympathy. Again and again I have been pleading—wherever I dared to plead—for patience; urging them to try to believe, even in the face of all they see, that the light can come, even into our proud British hearts. But they cannot believe it. And I have comforted myself with the thought: There is one Indian who will understand; Mr. Gandhi will see how an Englishman still has faith that his countrymen will see the right thing and do it—if only it is put to them in a way that will open their eyes. He who has shown such faith in his fellow countrymen that he thought them able to overcome evil without violence; who after many bitter disappointments still has faith in his own people, still strives and struggles to purify their national life; who refuses to be embittered or discouraged by their failure to respond: this man will understand. And he did.

I asked him what was my duty as an Englishman on my return to England. At first, not quite seeing what was in my mind, he replied: "Well, first we want you to get off our backs." His use of that sharp expression wounded me. It was what every other Indian had conveyed to me, but none quite so sharply. Perhaps he thought I, as an Englishman, would only understand an expression of that kind. Like other Indians I have met, his intuition worked a little too quickly, so that he overshot the mark. Yet I was glad afterwards to think that he had said that. It left no doubt of his sustained belief that the political subjection of India must first be ended. Unlike some other Indians I have met, he very quickly perceived what I really meant: that I accepted that first demand without difficulty; but that the difficulty arose in considering how the mind of Britain could be so changed as to perceive that we have become a burden on the back of India, and that we need not be and must not be so.

As I was explaining myself rather further another visitor arrived, an Indian, who made obeisance right to the floor, as if he had come into the presence of a god. I saw that Mr. Gandhi disliked this, and tried to ignore it. Also I noticed that the man was not wearing *khaddar*. It seemed sad that one who worshipped him as a god should still fail to do the first thing the Mahatma demands of his followers. But perhaps I misjudged him. I stopped speaking to give the newcomer his chance. But Mr. Gandhi encouraged me to go on. It took a little time to unburden myself, and the other man soon got impatient and interrupted (in Gujarati, of course). He probably found it preposterous that an English visitor should be allowed to speak thus to the Mahatma. I stopped again, but Mr. Gandhi spoke rather sharply to him and bade me continue.

I felt that I was doing too much of the talking, but he was most sympathetic. He warmly agreed that the real change needed is moral rather than just political; that we British have to learn national humility and put aside the thought that we have some national destiny to show other people how to live. He readily understood how keen an Englishman must be that his country should do right because it is right, and not just because of the pressure of events. And, what I cared for most, he seemed able to believe that the mind of Britain might change. Once I noticed he quoted Tolstoy, but I do not now remember the sense of the quotation.

When we had talked for nearly an hour Mr. Desai appeared and I left.

Next morning, when I came from my early breakfast, Mr. Gandhi was cutting up vegetables at a table, so I said he ought to give me a job like that to do, "Oh well," he said, "if you want to do this you must come in time; you must be here at a quarter-past six." So for the remaining three mornings I cut up vegetables with him from six to seven. The first morning he began by saying that it must seem strange to me as an Englishman that he sat in a chair while the ladies (there were three of them at work) stood up. Of course, I told him that I understood that he was bound to sit because of his health; but we had a nice talk about Eastern and Western standards of men's treatment of women, and especially the different ways in which we express the companionship of man and wife. I never spoke to Mrs. Gandhi, though she does speak a little English. I believe she several times told people in the kitchen to offer me more milk or what not; and she "took notice" when I was saying good-bye. She is a motherly woman, who is, I should think, a very good *hausfrau;* and she looks as if she had shared pretty fully the burdens that have fallen upon her husband's back. Yet I never saw them even exchange a glance. All the same, I am sure they know what is in one another's mind.

I think it was this conversation that led on to the fact that I was a Quaker. This excited Mr. Gandhi very much. He talked of his old friend Mr. Coates in South Africa thirty-five years ago (see the *Autobiography)*, and one or two others he knew well about the same time; but it is a very long time since he heard anything of him. And he spoke with great affection of Quakers generally, though he seems to have known few or none in recent years. He knew about William Penn, and the authoress of a recent big history of Pennsylvania gave him a copy. I found that all the members of the *ashram* who discovered I was a Quaker responded in just the same way—and with the same lack of actual knowledge.

The following morning was Mr. Gandhi's silent day, so we did our vegetable-cutting in silence; it happened to be a little awkward, as I found myself confronted with a big pumpkin or some such vegetable, and I did not know how to deal with it. I had only a small pocket-knife of my own to cut with; the four kitchen knives that are all the household possesses were pre-occupied by Mr. Gandhi and the ladies. However, I gradually learnt by observing the ladies. They did not speak English. It was an unusual kind of "silent meeting".

One of the members took me round the *khaddar* department one day. I have found it difficult to accept the economic validity of *khaddar;* but I am beginning to see it in a new light. I think we in the West have largely misunderstood it (it may not be entirely our own fault) by supposing that Mr. Gandhi's main idea was to revert from manufacture to hand-spinning. But to put it that way is to misunderstand his main purpose. To be sure, he has spoken again and again of the evils of factory life; and anyone who has had the smallest acquaintance with the factory life of India must admit that his criticisms are not exaggerated: they hardly could be. One purpose of the revival of hand-spinning is to save the people from the necessity of being dragged into factory life, but that is not its main purpose. Let Mr. Gandhi be his own witness: "The sole claim advanced on its behalf", he has written, "is that it alone offers an immediate, practicable, and permanent solution of that problem of problems that confronts India, viz. the enforced idleness for nearly six months of the year of the overwhelming majority of India's population, owing to lack of a suitable supplementary occupation to agriculture and the chronic starvation of the masses that results therefrom." In any case, I think those who are sceptical about *khaddar* as an economic proposition ought to read Gregg's *Economics of Khaddar* before they make up their mind. Its moral value is, I think, absolutely proved. There appears to be less drinking in the villages that have taken it up. And it is bringing professional men into intimate association with the villagers, helping to form a union of hearts; the bond of a common task surely forms one of the closest human ties.

The man from the Christa Seva Sangh at Poona told me he had been talking with Mr. Gandhi about their proposal for social work among the Poona students. Mr. Gandhi had shown himself unsympathetic. He seemed to have no use for work that would bring some humanizing influence into the students' life. He wants them to come right out of the Westernized colleges and to build new colleges with a new ideal. I cannot easily follow him here. It seems to me almost like refusing to succour soldiers because you disapprove of war. And apart from the demand of charity, surely if kindness is shown to the students they are more likely to listen to what may be said about new educational methods and ideals. But I did not discuss this personally with Mr. Gandhi. So perhaps I did not get his full meaning.

On Sunday afternoon a Christian student whom I had met at Poona last October came with a friend of his from Ahmedabad to see me. We had a good talk about Christians and communalism. I was delighted to find that their Ahmedabad Christian students' union arranges meetings with Christian and non-Christian speakers, and so tries to foster inter-communal fellowship. But they still had no good to say for the missionaries in Gujarat.

I had one or two little talks with Pandit Motilal Nehru while he was there. He is, I am afraid, incapable of believing any good of England. He thinks a nation that has grown strong by material things cannot go against self-interest, and he thinks a free India would destroy British trade. So India must wrest her freedom from an unwilling England.

The evening before I left the *ashram,* just at the end of our meal H. Q. noticed a snake. It proved to be a fine black cobra. So I have seen one live cobra in India.

During another meal a big grey monkey came and sat on its tail in the little garden, as if waiting for an audience. I do not know if Mr. Gandhi noticed it; but it went away disappointed.

My time at the *ashram* was all too short. I had been delayed in Delhi by a touch of fever and a horrid sore throat; and on my last day at Sabarmati, when I had planned to see the infants' school and the village reconstruction after the flood of last autumn, I was prostrated on my bed for most of the day. But if I did not see how Mr. Gandhi and his colleagues apply the method of Montessori, I at least saw a good many of the infants "out of school".

It happened that, as I was returning from a little bird-walk, wearing my binoculars, I met three small boys, so I offered them a look through the glasses, and of course they were wildly excited and pleased. An hour or two later, while I was resting in my room, a number of children appeared outside the window, and began pointing through the bars. It took me some little time to discover what they wanted. Of course, it was the binoculars. They had a great time with them; I think they really found more amusement by looking at one another through the wrong end, and seeing each other far away, than by looking the proper way through, which always involved a lot of tiresome readjustment of the eye-pieces. I think little children understand the minimizing better than the magnifying. I had no idea when I left home what a lot of delight my binoculars would cause. The children of the weavers' colony near Itarsi were the first to discover them last September; and I think the parents were as much fascinated as the children. The English children on the Rangoon–Calcutta boat got a lot of amusement out of them. All these Eastern children—most of the English ones even—seem much more patient in waiting for their turn than Western children. I suppose the climate makes them quieter.

The children at Sabarmati are obviously very happy; and the centre of their happiness is "Bapu" himself. Each day some of them accompany him on his walk. He marches briskly along with half a dozen children dancing along beside him, and the favoured one of the day (each in turn, I fancy) holds his hand.

The last morning during the vegetable cutting we discussed the difficult problem of Assam and its opium. He is pessimistic. He fears Assam cannot get rid of opium without financial assistance from the Central Government—that is to say, until military expenditure is reduced. As I was going he asked me to write to him whenever I had anything to write about; and he suggested my sending any criticisms concerning defects I had noticed in the *ashram*. My mind immediately turned to the absence of silence in the times of prayer—though what I said was that I was in no position to judge after such a short visit. "Oh, yes," he said, "for instance, you may have noticed this wet patch where people wash their hands after meals. We are so stingy that we have never had it properly drained. But I am hoping to see how to do it soon." What a mind he has for details! No wonder some Indians think him very Western.

Part of a letter written to me by Mr. Gandhi subsequently has an interesting bearing on this incident, and I think I may quote it. "You seem to think lightly of my having invited suggestions with reference to sanitary matters. In my own humble opinion we needlessly divide life into watertight compartments, religious and other. Whereas if a man has true religion in him it must show itself in the smallest details of life. To me sanitation in a community such as ours is based upon common spiritual effort. The slightest irregularity in sanitary, social, and political life is a sign of spiritual poverty. It is a sign of inattention, neglect of duty. Anyway, the *ashram* life is based upon this conception of fundamental unity of life."

Mr. Gandhi is a most lovable man. He makes it easy for a newcomer to treat him as an old friend, and I think he likes to be so treated instead of as a saint. After all, if he liked to be treated as a saint he would not be one. He insisted on shaking hands when we parted, though he knew by then that I understood something of Indian ways.

It is perhaps dangerous to estimate the place now held by Mr. Gandhi in India. His name is still in every mouth. He is not to-day an active political force; but he could be if he would. He is still the friend and adviser and sustainer of some of the most devoted leaders of the country. They turn to him in every hour of need. The people of the country still worship him. Few accept his demands: the spinning and wearing of *khaddar,* the removal of untouchability, complete abstinence, and non-violence in thought and deed. The boisterous, emotional acceptance of his leadership and his vows has gone; but the body of those who are seriously trying to carry out his principles seems to be growing steadily. From time to time a new victory over some evil custom is achieved by non-violent means; from time to time the violence of communal friction seems to decrease; but the belief in non-violent methods of dealing with the British does not grow at present.

It is not easy to sum up my impression of the *ashram.* One cannot but be aware of the contrast between this place and Santiniketan. The Satyagrahashram (the Soul-force Community) relies on a severe daily discipline, strict asceticism, and the regular performance of menial tasks; Gandhi is a strict Puritan. Tagore is a Poet. He relies on aesthetic expression, on releasing the soul of man, on silent meditation. Yet I think their goal is the same—or, at least, more nearly the same than either of them perhaps would admit. Tagore seems to doubt the efficacy of the way of renunciation, while Gandhi doubts the efficacy of the way of free growth. But it may well be that each method is needed for various types of men: Tagore will appeal to those men and women who are by nature individualist and revolutionary; Gandhi to the numbers who are attracted by a hard discipline—those who become Jesuits or join the army. The Servants of India are following yet another road—in some respects closely parallel to Mr. Gandhi's—to the same goal. All are leading to the growth of a strong, enlightened people, worthy to take the highest place in the brotherhood of men. They will have learned that only by self-discipline and by losing himself can man find his true life of harmony with his fellows. From such a death of self the new world culture is surely springing into life.

XII

BOMBAY
April 5, 1928

A good many things have happened since I left Mr. Gandhi's *ashram;* so at the risk of anti-climax I revert from India's great leader to her silent masses, to her hills and plains.

From Ahmedabad I went to Mount Abu, a little way north again, in Rajputana. My purpose was to meet Mr. Pope, the British Resident at Indore, who is president of a special committee, consisting chiefly of the representatives of Indian princes, who are considering how the smuggling of Malwa opium can be suppressed. Malwa opium is derived from poppy grown in various Rajput and Central Indian States. Its growth and manufacture are not under British control, and in recent years a great deal has got into the hands of smugglers.

Mount Abu is a hilly region rising to 5,000 feet. From Abu Road station a motor-bus takes you fifteen miles up the hills to the little town, about 3,500 feet up. The hills are very rocky; about half the landscape seems in places to consist of bare rock. The rest is tree-clad. The grass was all brown and withered, and most of the trees were leafless, so the hills looked rather dull and drab. But here and there were patches of green, including some quite fresh foliage; and in the higher parts the Flame of the Forest, a small tree with brilliant red flowers, was in gorgeous bloom. From about 3,000 feet, too, we came upon a flowering tree that suggested the almonds of the Riviera; actually the flower is more purple and larger, and the name of the tree is, I believe, *Bauhinia variegata.*

I had some delightful walks during my two days at Mount Abu. Two different roads led to the ridge, from which there was a great view across the flat desert country to the west. The heat was much less than at Ahmedabad, and there was always a cool breeze. Two Indians that I talked to separately assured me that Ahmedabad in April and May has the most intolerable climate to be found in India. That may be a picturesque exaggeration—but not much.

There are some wonderful Jain temples at Mount Abu, eight or nine hundred years old. They form a striking contrast to most Hindu temples. The temples of Benares or of South India are finely proportioned but lacking in beautiful detail, and to the unaccustomed Western eye ugly, even revolting, in much of the interior ornamentation. These Mount Abu temples are opposite in both respects. The outside is inconspicuous and unattractive. Inside is an immense wealth of exquisitely delicate and marvellously rich stone-carving, where one could wander for hours or days, feasting upon beauty and constantly making new discoveries. There are numbers of little shrines and some greater and holier ones, where the Western pagan may not penetrate; but the priest goes inside and lights a taper so that you may dimly see the wonders of the interior—you are expected chiefly to admire the costly jewels in the forehead of the squatting images. Why is the Westerner in the East supposed to be unable to appreciate anything except what is very costly? The real glory of these temples consists in the exquisite stone-carving on the roofs and the pillars. Well may it be said that they are as wonderful as the Taj—though the comparison is absurd. Yet they seem to be little known.

I travelled through the night to Bombay and, leaving my heavy luggage, went through the following night to spend a week-end in Itarsi and say good-bye to the Friends there. It was immensely interesting to revisit, after these seven months, the places that had given me my first impressions of India. The luxuriance of last September had given place to a deadly drought. In the autumn it seemed as if lots of land were wasted in little strips of pasture that ought to have been ploughed. Now one wondered how the cattle could keep alive at all on these dried-up strips. The cotton crop was nearly over and looked very dejected; the wheat had all been harvested and only stubble was left in the fields. Most of the jungle trees were bare, and the Flame of the Forest was nearly over. Round Itarsi itself unseasonable rains had ruined the wheat crop in February; they are having to take "famine" measures.

I had to travel by a later train than before, reaching Itarsi about two in the afternoon. By then the heat was intense, the shade temperature about 100^0 F., and the sun blazing and scorching from a cloudless sky. I longed for the great thunder clouds of September.

It had been a shock to go from the free and equal atmosphere of the Sabarmati *ashram* to the obsequiousness of Mount Abu, where every down-trodden Rajput, man and boy (not women), salaams and bows to the sahib, as if one were the Prince of Wales. And now, here at Itarsi, I was thrown right back into the mean squalor of agricultural India, from which Mr. Gandhi and many others, English as well as Indian, have striven and are striving to raise the country.

I think I must record one incident, for I came right into the middle of it. G. W. M. took me out into the jungle on Saturday afternoon, a few hours after I arrived. Our time was a good deal curtailed, as several visitors came with all sorts of odd requests just as we were starting. But we did get a peaceful half-hour away from humanity's claims, and it refreshed us both. As we were returning I noticed two men signalling to us; so we stopped and they came up. One was a schoolmaster. He had a sad tale to tell. During school that morning a boy—no longer attending school—had climbed up into a tree outside the school, and caused a very annoying "diversion". He refused to come down when ordered. When at last he did come down the master used his cane on him. Head teachers are allowed to cane their boys by the provincial regulations; but technically this boy was no longer under his jurisdiction.

When the head master went home he found the boy and his parents waiting for him outside his house. The mother tried to block the door, so he pushed her aside and she fell down. The father then rushed at him, but he avoided him, and the father stumbled and fell. He went into his house, and the infuriated family went away, breathing out fire and slaughter and threatening him with the police.

That was the schoolmaster's story. After some discussion G. W. M. thought it best to go with the schoolmaster and his friend to see the police inspector. I sat in the car while they talked, so I only heard the result afterwards. I should say, by the way, that the parents are "Christians", and they live in a house belonging to the mission, and have been making a nuisance of themselves in various ways lately. It appeared that the inspector had had a visit from the father; he said he had tried to dissuade him from taking any proceedings. So he heard the other side and took note that there was thought to be danger of a breach of the peace. He then asked if there was anything else against the man. G. W. M. said there was nothing definite, though I believe the schoolmaster afterwards mentioned something else. So the inspector remarked that there had been one or two robberies in Itarsi lately: he might threaten the man with the guilt of them!

I wonder what the ordinary Westerner will think of that remarkable proposal. It sounds to us like blackmail. And, of course, G. W. M. repudiated the idea. All the same, it strikes me that probably the inspector merely saw in it an easy way of getting a "just" settlement of a tiresome incident. No doubt he knew that the man was a bad man; here he was, trying to trump up a case against a comparatively innocent schoolmaster. What justice required was that the fellow should be put in his place. Here was a way to do it, a way that he would understand.

So the matter was left. On Sunday afternoon, just as we were going to tea with the G.s, the parents were standing outside to see G. W. M. He said he would be back in half an hour. They came later and talked the thing over without getting much farther. Of course, they had heard at once of our visit to the police.

I have described this incident fully because I believe it is typical of the kind of thing any mission in an "out-station" is coping with daily. Some of us live in a world of movements towards understanding and reconciliation between nations and classes. Perhaps we sometimes forget that vast numbers of our fellow beings have not yet learned how to live in peace with their next-door neighbours. It is, I fancy, becoming increasingly difficult for any Englishman to heal such a breach between Indians. His prestige is going or has gone, and it may be a handicap rather than a help to be English, because he cannot fully understand the point of view of the disputants, and because he is akin to the alien Government. He has nothing to rely on but his character. If he has earned the respect of his neighbours by his "daily life and conversation", good. If not, he can do little or nothing. It is a very great testimony to G.W. M. that the people do come to him, expecting him to help them.

Itarsi is a mushroom town of some ten thousand inhabitants; it has grown up round a railway junction and is still growing. It suffers from all the vices you expect in a new place. If there are any young Quakers who have a "concern" to make the world a little more heavenly than it is to-day, they might like to try their hand in Itarsi. If they can build the new Jerusalem there they can build it anywhere—even in Geneva.

I think there is still a place in India, as in all other countries, for people who are willing to share the love of God with the loveless, and ready to learn even from those who seem to have nothing to teach. There is no place in the world to-day for condescension; but humble service, whether of an Englishman in a squalid part of India or an Indian in a squalid part of England, brings its reward.

If only we could get rid of the incubus of an alien Government, Englishmen who are trying to be Christ's disciples would be welcome all over India. That is the conclusion I have reached. They could help India to do the things the alien Government has failed to do. And if they will really identify themselves with the life of India, as C. F. Andrews has done, they will be welcome without reserve even to-day.

I do not believe that the true disciples of Christ in the East to-day ought to be seeking for "converts". Of course there are plenty of people in India, as in the West, who need to be turned from darkness to light, from fear to love, from self to service; but baptism and Church membership cannot produce these things.

Too often those acts stand for hypocrisy and self-seeking. Christ-like lives seem to be the only force that can save the world.

Did I mention an Indian Christian (who formerly stayed with Father Tyrrell in Birmingham and visited George Cadbury) whom I met in Delhi? He began by assuring me that it was impossible for an Englishman to be a Christian, at any rate in India. Then he said, "We don't want missionaries who come to India and take part in politics." "But surely", I said, "you don't object to Mr. Andrews, do you?" "Oh, no," he replied, "he isn't a politician. By political missionaries we mean those who support the Government. Mr. Andrews's work is social reform, not politics." I found it rather amusing to contrast this with those dear folk in England who condemn us for being "political" whenever we try to hasten some social reform that the Government is hindering.

I have not much more to say about Itarsi. On Saturday evening G.W. M. took me with half a dozen of the Indian Friends to an hour of prayer together, lying out under the stars in the open fields. I was tired, and slept before the end. I felt akin to the heavy-eyed disciples of long ago under those same springtime stars in Palestine.

It was comforting to be at a Friends' meeting again on Sunday. It was the kind of meeting that might have caused me to blaspheme in England. It was mostly prearranged, and the free time was taken up with long-winded prayers. That is the stage these good people have reached. But to be in a place where even a measure of freedom was allowed for the Spirit (perhaps the "carnal mind", too) to blow where it would was refreshing to a parched soul that has only had one Quaker meeting since September.

The afternoon was spent in the jungle again with the G.s, and on Monday morning I had my last bird-walk in India, and added two to my long list of Indian birds. In the jungle the *mhowa*-tree was just shedding its flowers. They are rather sickly but very succulent, and I am not surprised that the people use them for toddy. I have not experimented in the taste or other effects of opium; the nearest I have come to experience the drug and drink habits of the East was to chew the unfermented *mhowa* in the Itarsi jungle.

Then back to Bombay, in the company of a pleasant Indian youth who "travels" for the Imperial Tobaccoo Company and smoked a good many "Gold Flakes" as part of his business. Unhappily for him he failed with his fellow passengers. Another Indian, travelling in tea, who joined us for a time, found we were all addicted to his drug. There are not very many Indian "commercials" and I had not met them before. The tea traveller was very sorry of himself: they never get a holiday and they work seven days a week. If they ask for a day off they are told they need not come back. Contrary to custom, it was the fat man who bewailed his fate, while the lean young man sat and laughed good-humouredly at this tale of woe. Finally the tea-seller prevailed on me to play chess with him, a game I have hardly played for years; and he beat me twice, so he went away in peace. His method of play was to seize some minor piece by a subterfuge, and then start a process of frightful slaughter, till I was left with a king and a pawn or two, and he had an extra piece and perhaps an extra pawn. Only he had no idea how to avoid stalemate, and I had to finish the game for him.

In the dining-car I talked to an ancient white-bearded Catholic missionary, perhaps South German, who is retiring to Ireland after thirty-five years in India. He was very scornful of people who visit India for a few months and then write books: "That Miss Mayo," he said: "she was in India for six months and then wrote a book that is full of mistakes." He was afraid he would die if there was snow in England; so I told him Ireland was milder—and wetter.

When I got back to Bombay I was given a room to share with a Canadian missionary doctor from Central India (from one of the very small States), and I immediately discovered that he knew all about opium—or, at least, a great deal. His medical knowledge was a most useful supplement to Mr. Pope's information. Of course, like every sane man, he admitted that a great many people take opium for fifteen or twenty years without any visible effect. But even these moderate consumers are often neglecting their children because they must have the drug; They may be affectionate parents and husbands, but the drug kills their moral sensibility. That is just the sort of thing that even a good official does not know, because he has not the opportunity to see it. But the doctors know. This doctor was the first man I have met in India who has tried to cure opium addicts (it is noteworthy that they want to be cured). It was very interesting to compare his experience with what I have heard in Java and Malaya. He has had a few real cures. He also told me one or two things that, as he said, were worse than anything in *Mother India.*

My last morning in Bombay has been spent in the company of a Servant of India, visiting the horrible *chawls* or one-room tenements, in which the population that drifts in from the starving country to work in the mills is housed. Some are just pig-sties; even the Government tenements are horrible enough; and the rents of the last lot put up by Government are so high that most remain empty. Many of those that are occupied are shared by several families. Except in the rains, the men mostly sleep outside. What happens during the rains I cannot imagine. Mr. G. (mine host) was pointing out to me last evening, as we came back late from seeing a Customs official and observed the sleeping forms along the pavements, that it is an unheard-of thing for an Indian woman to sleep out. That degradation is reserved for Mother England.

We ended our morning's tour of observation at the Social Service League centre—a delightful place where there are green grass and trees, where mothers get free dispensary treatment for their babies, where women get sewing lessons and men learn the technique of their trades, and many other excellent things happen: drama, and other joys of the soul.

India is an unhappy land—unhappy and at the same time fascinating. She has a freedom of the soul—a freedom from the tyranny of convention—that seems to me to lie deeper than our political freedom, deeper even than our "freedom of thought" in the West. And there are brave men and women in the land who, having true religion in their souls, will conquer the evils of the past and the present. Farewell to the country of our poor relations—poor in substance, but rich in affection.

XIII

Arabian Sea

April 6th—and after

Early this morning the coppersmiths were calling "Tonk! tonk! tonk!" as I have heard them daily for the past six weeks; the green parrots flew screaming over the *maidan;* I saw my last sun-bird in a Bombay garden. Along by the sea Parsees were standing on the shore saying their prayers. Farther out cattle egrets and reef herons stood statuesque on the mud, whilst gull-billed terns flitted lightly over the water. I lingered till the sun got too hot for my comfort.

Terns and gulls still flew round us as we left the harbour; then they disappeared and the life of India was left behind.

How odd it seems to be entirely among my fellow countrymen again! On the boat I know some American missionaries: one of whom I met in October at Nagpur, the others I met yesterday. Almost everyone else is British—the British of India. I am like a fish out of water. Now I must violently readjust myself to English customs, after having imbibed Indian preferences as well as I could for some months. It is hard work. The second evening on board I found myself trying to defend my fellow countrymen in face of the criticism of a quiet, sober-minded American. He has never been among English in the mass before. He has seen them as individuals—administrators or missionaries—in India; and he has conceived a very high respect for them. Now he sees them in bulk. He finds them (I should say "us") cold, surly, and ill-mannered. An Englishman at his table never deigns to speak to him unless he wants to let off some ignorant gibe at America. I suppose the truth is that the English Imperialist, especially the common half-educated type, suffers not so much from race or colour prejudice as from national prejudice: he has an unconscious, inordinate pride in being English, so he treats an American just as he would treat any other inferior "native". I tried to tell my American friend that we English are like that on the surface; but if he is patient he will find we are much better underneath.

It was good for me to have to defend my fellow countrymen. In India, when one hears criticism (I really heard very little), one has usually to remain speechless with shame. Criticism from an American one can stand up to.

The thaw sets in quickly. Before we are half-way across the Indian Ocean I find myself, unsociable by nature and dead-weary as I am of meeting new people, on friendly or at least speaking terms with half the people at my table and with a quarter of the other passengers. My cabin companion proves to be a broad-minded man (Irish, of course!) who has knocked about in the East for twenty years, has refused to lie down under convention, and who really cares to know even what *I* think about India. He does not, like most Western people I have met in India, lick his chops with satisfaction over *Mother India.* The *facts* may be true; but why should not Indians have different sins from ours if they like? The book is just an appeal to Western prejudice. He has evidently learned how to get Indians to work without bullying them.

I do not find many more to whom I can talk about India. They have the conventional views. But, away from politics, they are simple, amiable people. Probably I am thought to be more "standoffish" than most people because of my unfortunate inability to play games. Before we reach Port Sudan my American friend confesses that there are some very decent people on the boat; they seem much more friendly than he thought at first. Moreover, he and his colleagues are so good at joining in with games—in fact, such "good sports"—that the anti-missionary prejudice of the ordinary Britisher in the East gets a severe shock. The common idea about missionaries is very odd. That evening when I was trying to explain English mentality to the American missionary there happened to be a dance. Suddenly the first officer comes along: "Now then, you fellows, come along and help with the dance instead of talking religion all the time!"

There have been times when I wanted to sneak away from my fellow white men and settle down below among the Indian third-class passengers. But I have not done it. They might not know any English. In the evening I have hung over the railing and watched and listened for long, while a Sikh reader intones his scriptures in a loud voice, the others of his religion lying or sitting around passively listening. One day, when we swarmed all over the boat on a treasure hunt, I think our Indian fellow passengers got a curious sidelight on the manners and customs of the English. They stood silently gazing at our strange behaviour—commotion without passion or purpose. Perhaps they do not understand that in our cool climate nature puts a premium on physical alertness. The desire to escape from the stifling pressure of growing things by passive contemplation belongs only to the Tropics. They and we alike are creatures of our environment. This truth only dawned on me as I was reading Keyserling's *Travel Diary* on the boat; as soon as I read it I recognized it as truth—it is surely a truth of immense significance. Nature has forced us in the north to believe in the duty of hard work. Nature, likewise, has forced the inhabitant of the Tropics to live quietly, to conserve his energies. Our strenuous life has led us to marvellous scientific developments, to the mastery of many natural forces, to an elaborate economic organization. But the real end of all this progress is to release man's spirit from material and physical preoccupations to learn more of truth. The tropical man, having a more favourable natural environment, has been content to live a simpler life. In Africa this seems to have led to spiritual stagnation; not so in Southern Asia. We should think twice before insisting that those who have already advanced so far in knowledge and perception must accept our tradition of violent activity and elaborate social organization. We may reasonably urge that knowledge of truth must be partial and one-sided if it lacks understanding of natural law; and this, I think, the East is more and more disposed to recognize. But is the West prepared also to recognize that the truths of phenomena do not form the whole of reality?

Naturalists have a great advantage when travelling about the world. The expanse of ocean is not dull when at any moment you may see some scarce-known petrel from Oceania pass the ship, or come on deck to find the sea dotted with parties of phalaropes, soon to be off on their journey over desert and tundra to the Arctic coasts. Port Sudan is reputed a dreary spot; but it is not so to a man who watches a pratincole five yards away in the public garden, and finds a small bush at dusk packed so full of yellow wagtails, roosting before the next stage of their northern journey, that it seems to be ablaze with golden blossoms. All the time in India I have seen no nest with eggs; but here in the scrub near the lighthouse, within a stone's throw of the docks, I put a little warbler off the softest little domed nest, lined with white down or feathers and containing three pink eggs. And there are queer little black-throated doves feeding on the quay that suddenly shoot off across the harbour as if propelled from a catapult. And vultures are squatting calmly here and there, careless of man's presence, or soaring aloft. Port Sudan reveals to me a scientific fellow passenger, a learned man who can tell me all about the flora and fauna of deserts.

When we are through the Suez Canal I shall lose the soaring kites and vultures; but what does that matter if in a few days I can listen to the songs of scores of willow- and wood-warblers on the Lickey Hills?

Here am I, who have lived in Kent most of my life, and I never knew till to-day how ravishingly beautiful Kent could be. Those green meadows, and the tender blue of the Wealden Hills, and the orchards bursting into blossom! My eyes have been starved all these months, feeding only on exotic glories or dark seas or blinding deserts. Here is their natural food again. Such ravenous feasting on earth's beauty is painful. But it is an exquisite pain. England is a good place for an Englishman to live in.

Some Englishmen cannot live in England. They must find work away from home. They must make the best of it. And the sons of England have shown a rare ability for training people of other races who are as children to begin to grow up. As long as the children admire their tutors all is well; but the day comes when the youth begins to fret under tutorial control. That is the testing time. In the East many English people have stood the test none too well. They have become resentful. Why will not the Indians remain good children? Why are they so ungrateful to their tutors? Why do they accuse us of evil motives? Why do not they grow up nice, polite young men? If that is all we can say to India to-day, our task there is done. We can no longer rule India against the will of her two million (or is it ten million?) educated sons. There is only one honest course: it needs bold statesmanship and rare imagination; but it is not impossible. We must yield what they crave, yield full responsibility. No one knows what would follow, though most Englishmen think they know. There might be invasion from the north-west; there might be inter-communal or inter-state fighting; there might be renewed oppression of outcastes; there might be worse famine and plagues than to-day. Or there might not. Of one thing we can be quite sure. Whatever chaos might follow British withdrawal, there would be no reconquest of India by some other Power, say Japan. International jealousy and the growing enlightenment that finds expression in the League of Nations have together foiled Japanese and other ambitions in China. They would be no less effective for protecting India. There seem to be only two alternatives: to yield full responsibility, or to rule by the sword. The third way, the way of gradually increasing responsibility of Indians in partnership with British, is blocked; for the leaders of India will not co-operate. If we are not prepared to rule by the sword we must withdraw. Or, rather, we must come to an agreement with the moral leaders of India and accept their terms. And the British business community in India must prepare to face the consequences. For, if we go on as to-day, we must recognize that we are asking our administrators to do an impossible thing. There are Englishmen who are ever ready to face the impossible; and many no doubt will still go to India knowing they are going to face an impossible task—or not knowing it. If there is a catastrophe I venture to think that the British business community that has interests in India should bear the chief blame.

If, on the other hand, we do the bold, imaginative thing; if, putting aside force or the threat of force, we honestly ask the acknowledged leaders of India to meet our representatives on equal terms, to make a treaty of friendship between India and Britain, I believe we shall find that their terms will be surprisingly easy. Treat educated Indians as inferiors and we shall get nothing but resentment and ever louder explosions of violence. Treat them with respect and consideration and with the candour due to equals, and we shall easily reach an agreement. It sounds easy, but it means breaking with a tradition that is deeply rooted, more deeply rooted than anyone can realize who has not been in India.

My Indian friends will not all accept this analysis. Some will say they never were children; they will say that the English never were disinterested tutors. I do not argue these points. The Indians may be right. The past is open to varied interpretations; the present is our chief concern.

Britain has never had a bigger political and moral issue to face than the issue in India to-day. She has had bitter lessons in America, in Canada, in Ireland, in South Africa: bitter lessons, but some were understood in time. Is there a Campbell-Bannerman in Britain to-day?